T0208719

# Into
# **Africa**

A Journey to the
Heart of Pokot

Jane Hamilton

WESTBOW
P R E S S®
A DIVISION OF THOMAS NELSON
& ZONDERVAN

Copyright © 2019 Jane Hamilton.

All rights reserved. No part of this book may be used or reproduced by any means,
graphic, electronic, or mechanical, including photocopying, recording, taping or by
any information storage retrieval system without the written permission of the author
except in the case of brief quotations embodied in critical articles and reviews.

Scripture taken from the New King James Version®. Copyright © 1982
by Thomas Nelson. Used by permission. All rights reserved

WestBow Press books may be ordered through booksellers or by contacting:

WestBow Press
A Division of Thomas Nelson & Zondervan
1663 Liberty Drive
Bloomington, IN 47403
www.westbowpress.com
1 (866) 928-1240

Because of the dynamic nature of the Internet, any web addresses or links contained in
this book may have changed since publication and may no longer be valid. The views
expressed in this work are solely those of the author and do not necessarily reflect the
views of the publisher, and the publisher hereby disclaims any responsibility for them.

Any people depicted in stock imagery provided by Getty Images are models,
and such images are being used for illustrative purposes only.
Certain stock imagery © Getty Images.

ISBN: 978-1-9736-4956-4 (sc)
ISBN: 978-1-9736-4958-8 (hc)
ISBN: 978-1-9736-4957-1 (e)

Library of Congress Control Number: 2018915024

Print information available on the last page.

WestBow Press rev. date: 02/12/2019

I dedicate this book to my husband, Dick Hamilton, whose vision and faith were far greater than mine, whose love for Jesus surpassed his human failings and whose life left a legacy in Pokot land that will reach into eternity.

# Contents

"If I rise on the wings of the dawn, if I settle on the far side of the sea, even there your hand will guide me, your right hand will hold me fast." **Psalm 139:9-10**

NIV

# Chapter 1

# A Night in Rome

Trust in the Lord with all your heart and lean not on your
own understanding; In all your ways acknowledge Him,
and He shall direct your paths.
Proverbs 3:5-6

*July 1976*

At midnight in an airport waiting room in Rome, three white faces seemed
out of place in a crowded room of Africans. A stocky red-haired man, a
teenage boy, and a quietly weeping woman (an obvious embarrassment
to the other two) waited for news of their delayed flight. Hour after weary
hour passed. Cold hard seats with unyielding arms denied exhausted bodies
any hope of rest. The small dimly lit waiting room and the musty smell
of travelers too long on the road added to the oppressive feel of the long
wait. Announcements came at regular intervals of yet another delay of a
flight destined to Nairobi, Kenya, including a stop at the airport in Entebbe,
Uganda, where a daring Israeli commando raid had just rescued 103 Jewish
hostages held by Idi Amin.

Sitting in that waiting room a terrible struggle waged inside me. It
was my first international trip, as we were headed to Kenya for missionary
service. My two male family members were doing the sophisticated world-
traveler thing, but I was in a melt down, terrified of what might be awaiting
us at the Entebbe airport. I desperately wanted to refuse to board that
flight. I just wanted to be safe back home in my long-gone living room. But
here I was, far from home, with my faith faint and my fears rising. With
visions of an enraged Idi Amin looking for vengeance on any white person,
my imagination was running wild. Looking around the waiting room,
wondering what was going on behind all those expressionless black faces

(we were to be the only whites on the flight), my anxiety and tears would not stop. My two macho companions would not even consider the risks. Cowed into silence, I settled into the comfort of quiet inside prayers and waited out the long night.

In the wee hours of the morning an announcement finally came that our flight would not land in Entebbe because the Israeli raid had disabled the tower. To my surprise, the whole waiting room erupted into loud applause and cheers. It turned out our fellow travelers were not Ugandans; they were Kenyans and, like us were headed to Nairobi, definitely not wanting to go to Entebbe in the aftermath of the raid. Only three black nuns in full habit got up and shuffled out in response to the call for a rescheduled Ugandan flight. I felt more than sheepish at my suspicions of our traveling companions. What a way to begin our missionary journey and what a valuable life lesson for me!

For three green missionaries it was a long night, and only one of many unsettling and sometimes terrifying nights that would be linked to the infamous Idi Amin, after we began our mission work just a stone's throw from the Uganda border.

We learned later that one of the hostages, an elderly Jewish woman who had been taken to the hospital, was killed in retaliation for the raid. Such was the brutality of Idi Amin.

Later, as a more seasoned and aware traveler, I know that *nothing* would have kept me from changing my flight to avoid that Entebbe landing. Fortunately, God took care of the problem. We came to realize later on that He did that quite often.

> Have I not commanded you? Be strong and of good courage;
> do not be afraid, nor be dismayed, for the LORD your God
> is with you wherever you go. (Joshua 1:9)

# Chapter 2

---

# The Calling – A Plane Crash and a Changed Life

I heard the voice of the Lord saying: "Whom shall I
send, and who will go for Us?" Then I said, "Here am I!
Send me."
Isaiah 6:8

How in the world did I find myself on the way to Africa? The timid soul inside of me, akin to Eeyore, would have pled, "No, Lord, not Africa!" and "No, Lord, not snakes!"

It all started on a routine Saturday afternoon in 1966. As a working mom, it was laundry and cleaning day. The kids had been outside playing when they came running into the house shouting, "Daddy just flew over the house and waved at us." "Sure he did," I said. (Dick owned a Chevron station and garage and was at work that day.) "Daddy is at work and he is not in an airplane buzzing the house."

Some hours later I was to learn that daddy had indeed been in an airplane buzzing the house.

A friend of Dicks learning to be a crop duster had rented a plane and they were out joy riding, but the joy ride turned to tragedy when they buzzed a lake to see if any buddies were fishing, and the hot afternoon air kept the plane from making the climb up out of the lake basin and over the ridge. A big old dead tree, top scarred by lightening, stuck up alone at the top of a ravine. The bottom of the plane hit the old stub of the tree, the gas line ruptured and the engine died. By this time they had cleared the ridge and were gliding. Dick could smell gas and was afraid of fire so as soon as they hit the tree tops he opened his door and jumped. Later his sister and brother-in-law found pieces of his shirt hanging forty feet up in the trees.

The first I knew that Dick had been in the plane was a phone call from a ham radio buff who had heard that a plane had gone down and that Dick Hamilton was one of the men on board. Mercy Flights was picking them up and flying them to Medford. That was all the caller knew. I rushed to the nearest hospital and waited. The pilot was brought in on a stretcher in serious condition. No one knew what had happened to the other guy in the plane. Long agonizing hours later I learned that he was alive.

The pilot had stayed with the plane and suffered permanent injuries. Dick's side of the plane was buried in the ground. If he had stayed in the plane he probably would have been killed. Dick survived the jump with only brush burns, broken ribs and superficial injuries. Unable to get the jammed doors of the plane open to get to his unconscious buddy, Dick ran to the nearest road and flagged down a car. The driver had heard the plane come down and was looking for the crash site. After other help arrived and the pilot was loaded into the Mercy Flights plane, Dick declined to get in the plane. I guess he had had enough flying for one day. He was brought home by vehicle and went to a small private hospital where my mom was a nurse. That was where I finally tracked him down.

The young assistant pastor from our church visited him in the hospital and told him that God must have some special job in mind for Him to have spared his life. Dick was sure he had saved himself by jumping. He wasn't much into God's providence at that point in his life; that would come later.

Soon after the plane crash God began to work in Dick's life. He was basically a good guy who believed in God, but he loved everything wild and challenging and difficult, from drift boating the Rogue River to motorcycling with buddies during his police force days, and building and racing stock cars. If those things took him away from family on nights and weekends, then that was just how it was. There were years of struggling, with me trying to keep the young ones interested in church even if Dad was going fishing and doing more "fun" things.

Then, after fourteen years of marriage, things began to change. Only it was not as I had envisioned it in my prayers. God does things His own way, and in His own time. It was the plane crash and the events that followed. It was God putting people in the right place and right time to do the outreach. It was the time that the drinking was supposed to stop for the "make up" period, and he could not stop. It was Dick getting out of the car and onto his knees at 3:00 a.m. on the way home from a bar and asking God for help. In finding that he did not have the power to change his life on his own, Dick knew where the power could be found. He turned his life over to Jesus who specializes in changing lives. God did a wonderful work in turning him around and setting his feet on a new path. God changed his life completely.

Then God had to do some changing in my life. I had been the *spiritual* one in our family for so long that I set about to give Dick the benefit of all my years of church. God had to bring me up short and show me that I was not a stepping-stone but a stumbling block and I had to get out of the way. I was *not* to be the spiritual head of our family. God worked through my brother, John Heberling, who was the minister at our home church, and through their Wednesday noon prayer-instead-of-lunch times. After Dick became active in the church, John took him to a missionary convention in Portland, Oregon. The rest is history.

Hamilton family, Pre-Africa

Dick, Jane, Carolee, Gram Heb, Rick and Tiffany

Dick in his *Little Spook* drift boat, lining up to shoot the
infamous Blossom Bar Rapids on the Rogue River.

Dick's passion for stock car racing and white water boating transitioned
into a passion for the gospel of the Lord Jesus. His favorite saying:
"It's not fair for people to hear the gospel over and over when there
are people in the world who have not heard it the first time."

# Chapter 3

# Going but Not Knowing

By faith Abraham obeyed when he was called ... And he
went out, not knowing where he was going.
Hebrews 11:8

I knew early on that I had married into an adventure. I so loved this guy, from
the red-headed farm boy I had first encountered in a little fifth grade school
room, to the grown-up dare devil, ready-for-anything man, I had always
loved him and prayed for him to surrender his life to the Lord. But I had no
idea where that decision would lead us. From the time Jesus got a hold on
his life, it was full speed ahead. Dick was totally grasped and motivated by a
strong call of God that never wavered through forty years of trial and testing.
When I dragged my feet about going into the wilds of Africa, his teasing
comment was: "If Moses had waited for his wife to make up her mind, the
children of Israel would still be in Egypt." He was sure of his calling and was
sure that he and God made up a majority.

My vision had always been having him next to me in the pew on Sunday
mornings. Dick's vision was to find an unreached people who had never
heard the word of God. And so we went. . . into the unknown. . . into an
adventure beyond anything I could have imagined.

For we walk by faith, not by sight. (2 Corinthians 5:7)

*Letting Go*

The decision and the *letting go* did not come easy for me, but what my friend
calls "divine coincidences" began to happen. Unsure that I really wanted to
sell my dream house, I put a tiny ad in the classifieds. The first people that
came to look at the house had cash money from a sale in California and my

house was gone. I had grown up moving from one shabby rental to another, with a single mom and three brothers, and my dream had always been to have a home of my own. So when Dick's business was good, we planned and built a house with all our wants and wishes, from wallpaper to wainscoting and a beautiful white limestone fireplace. We had been in my dream home for seven years and now it was all going away from me. Everything was moving and shaking under my feet. So many mornings I pulled out of our driveway and cried all the way to my desk in the customer service department at Harry and David Gourmet Gifts. But I knew deep down that I was only a pawn in a bigger game, and so it played on. Dick's race car had not even been advertised when someone knocked on our door one morning and wanted to buy the race car and the little junk yard of spare parts hidden behind the fence. Those *coincidences* just kept happening until I knew it was in the Lord's will for us to GO. My part was just to surrender my will to God's will and to try to keep up with the current that was carrying us along.

The first step was two years of Bible College for Dick in Seattle. There I found a wonderful job in the home office of Safeco Insurance doing marketing and working on conferences and trips for the highest ranking insurance agents nation wide. It was a dream job but I had to keep reminding myself that I was just passing through. Then there were the years of traveling to the churches seeking financial support. For people who were "do it yourself" types, it was a humbling experience, but it taught us one valuable lesson. We were not doing this on our own. God was involved providing the needed support, from the least expected places and a lot of very small gifts from very many people, adding up to a living link support to get us on our way. Receiving the "widow's mite" is a very sobering thing. It was all part of the process of God preparing us with humble hearts and grateful souls.

Early on God showed us that the support comes from Him, not from our meager fundraising efforts. Our two home churches at Central Point and Medford, Oregon, rallied around as our supporting/sending congregations and the elders of the two churches formed our Board of Directors. They continued as our life line for forty years. As we prepared to go we had packed our things and purchased a Toyota Land Cruiser to ship with our household goods. As the time came to depart we still needed $7,000 to pay for the shipping. I set about writing letters to our sponsors to "raise" the needed funds.

God had other plans. A long-time church friend of mine had a sister who was married to the missions chairman at the Myrtle Point Christian Church and they wanted a mission presentation. We had no supporters there so Dick went alone to share the Kenya work and I stayed home to write support letters. In God's provision, Dick came home with a check for $7,000, the tithes from a logging operation run by a couple of the church leaders. That was the first of many times that God provided in amazing ways for the needs at the critical time, from His own sources out of the wealth of His people, often before we even knew the emergency or the need was coming. God is good. It was a confirmation of His partnership with us and always a comfort to know that God had our backs.

With all the preparation done, we shipped our barrels and crates and off we went... to a far corner of the earth, a place that time had forgotten. Little did I know the heights and depths to which that journey would take us.

> The will of God will not take you where the grace of God cannot keep you. (Anon)

# Chapter 4

## Falling Through a Time Crack
## . . and Finding it Home

If I rise on the wings of the dawn, if I settle on the far side
of the sea, even there your hand will guide me, your right
hand will hold me fast
Psalm 139:9-10 (NIV)

After our eventful flight, we settled into language school in Nairobi, the beautiful "green city in the sun" that is the capital of Kenya. We studied Swahili, Kenya's national language, since the Pokot language was hardly written at the time. At school break, we welcomed the chance to escape and set out across country to visit our new home. Dick had gone to Africa on a survey trip in 1974 looking for a place where people had not heard the name of Jesus. By some amazing contacts through MAF pilot, Arnie Neuman and an African pastor named George Kendagor, God led him into the untouched bush of North Pokot. For our son Rick and for me, this trip would be our first look at the place that God and Dick had chosen.

We loaded up *Big Red*, our Toyota Land Cruiser, crossed the equator and traveled out across the beautiful highlands of Kenya, awed by the landscape of lush green patchwork fields, clumps of banana trees, little thatched roof huts, gorgeous skies and the picturesque flat-topped thorn trees that dot the countryside like huge umbrellas. It was the *White Highlands* where early British settlers had farmed and lived *the good life*. The landscape was breathtaking. Then we came to the edge of the Great Rift Valley and headed down the steep 2,000 foot escarpment into the valley floor.

The rock and dirt road, mostly one lane, hugged the side of the mountain with turn-outs for on coming traffic but we never saw another vehicle on the whole trip. Reaching the valley at the bottom was like falling through a time crack; no lush green fields, no banana trees, only the monotonous brown vegetation of the flat arid bush land along the Kenya-Uganda border. The only road through the area was a narrow dirt road that was sometimes not much more than a goat trail. Frequent drainage gullies that cut across the road made shifting into low gear a regular event, the Land Cruiser bucking and swaying down into the *wadi* and struggling up the other side. The only sign of life we saw was the occasional bare backside of a man quickly disappearing into the bush at the sound of our approaching vehicle. I looked around dismayed wondering how *anyone* could live in this desolate place.

A real step of faith is getting out of the car in the desert when your bladder says it can't take one more bump in the road and you no longer care what might be lurking behind that roadside bush. After eleven hours, several "bush breaks" and late in the darkest of nights (no electric lights, no gas stations, no shops, nothing but that endless teeth-rattling bumpy road), we finally came to the little house of Pastor Andrew Kendagor, an African missionary living deep in the bush among the Pokot people. Andrew and his Pokot wife were trying to begin an outreach into the nomadic warrior culture of the Pokot tribe. Andrew's father, Pastor George Kendagor, was the man who first took Dick into Pokot territory and showed him the needs of the people who were untouched by civilization or by the gospel message.

Pastor Andrew and his little tribe of kids welcomed us. (It was always hard to figure out which kids were his and which were strays he had taken in, but he always had a houseful.) To the light of a kerosene lantern we threw our sleeping bags on the floor of his house, exhausted and ready for sleep. Too hot to crawl inside, we sprawled out on top of the sleeping bags. Then, just as we were dozing off, the heavens opened and pounding rain, like a hundred drums on the tin roof above our heads, announced the beginning of the rainy season.

Nine months of the year Pokot land is dry and brown. For three months the rains bring about 8 to 12 inches of badly needed rain for the cattle and people, transforming the brown vegetation into beautiful multi shades of green and blanketing the desert floor with tiny flowers. That first night for us in Pokot land the rains came with a terrific force.

Andrew's house was a typical bush house like the African huts except that it was square and had a roof made of corrugated tin sheets. The rough walls were mud, plastered over a frame of lumber woven with tree branches.

The floors were made of packed mud mixed with cow dung. During the dry season that concoction makes a nice hard, shiny, sweep-able floor, but in the pounding rain, with a leaking roof, we found ourselves sliding about on slippery sleeping bags on the muddy cow dung floor. Dick slept soundly, as he always had an innate ability to do in *any* situation, but Rick and I were awake long into the night. With the smell of damp cow dung in our nostrils and the pounding rain on the roof, we laid our plans of how we would talk Dad out of his insanity. I assured Rick, "In the morning we'll talk about this and we'll go back up there to the beautiful green highlands and work among the people with the banana trees."

Laying there in the darkness I was overwhelmed by ghosts from the past as feelings came creeping up from a long buried childhood memory. It was1945. The war had just ended and so had my parents' marriage. My mom got on a bus in Pennsylvania with three kids and six suitcases headed for Oregon, a continent away. I was a little six year old traveling cross country by bus, feeling lost and lonely, knowing that life would never be the same again in that strange new place called Oregon. We arrived late one dark rainy night to a Greyhound bus depot, cold and dank, with no one there to meet us, and me wishing I could wake up from a bad dream and be back home in my own bed. Thirty years later, my first night in the African bush, I had that same lost feeling of displacement and wondering if I would ever feel any joy in this place

Waking up the next morning with that emptiness gnawing inside of me, I was waiting for an opportunity to talk to Dick about getting us out of there. Then Andrew's wife and kids came in bringing us a big metal tea pot of steaming chai (sweet tea brewed in milk) and a tray of huge enamel cups. It was a wonderful breakfast and it initiated in us a life-long love of African chai.

The bright African sun came out and we laid the muddy sleeping bags on the car to dry. My *talk* with Dick would have to wait.

The warm welcoming sun brought steam from the damp ground and brightened our way as Andrew walked us down a path to a little school room made of tin roofing sheets. There in that dark tin building was a small group of semi-naked boys learning their ABCs by writing in the dirt floor with sticks. It was the only school operating in an area with over 50,000 people. I stood there that morning transfixed, looking into the big brown eyes of those boys, eyes filled with amazement as they looked on the first white people they had ever seen. There was something in their eyes and expectant faces that touched deep inside of me, and somehow I never got around to telling Dick that we could not live and work in that desolate, forsaken place. After that day I never looked back.

Some of the boys from that small group grew up to be evangelists and pastors. A couple of them graduated from college and one went on to earn his PhD, this from among a people with less than five percent literacy rate.

That mysterious "thing" that grabbed my heart there in that little school room on that morning took me through forty years of loving and caring about the Pokot people. It carried me through a famine with so many tiny bodies with stick arms and legs and the sad, sad eyes of dying children. It took me through a deadly cholera epidemic when we covered the floor of the school building in sand for desperately ill people laid out like logs, hooked to IVs, spewing vomit and diarrhea simultaneously, and the staff with shovels scooping it up and throwing it down the latrines. Not knowing just how contagious it really was, we could only pray. Hundreds died in the bush during the cholera epidemic but not one person was lost at the mission.

Then there were the years of tribal warfare, gun shots in the night and constant uncertainty. What would cause a person to want to live like that? And, crazy as it sounds, to **like** it? How could one have peace and security in the midst of that kind of life? The only answer I ever had was that God's love constrained us and maintained us. There was no logical reason, nothing that made any sense, but often what God calls us to do does not make sense. What was that *thing* that grabbed me there in that little school room? Nothing but the Holy Spirit could have galvanized my life like that. Only the engulfing love of Jesus could have kept me going and given me that "peace that passes understanding."

Jesus calls us to walk in His steps, to practice the kind of love He showed us. Thomas said he would not believe unless he saw the marks in Jesus' hands, the marks of love that showed that He had given his life. The world is looking at the church. They are looking to see if those marks of love are there, the marks that will make the world recognize that we are His. Sometimes love costs. We open up and reach out. And wham! Someone rejects us, misunderstands us, or doesn't return our friendship. We are hurt. We don't want to open up next time. But this is what Jesus calls us to do, the higher form of love that makes you reach out, again and again, even when someone hurts you. . . the neighbor. . . someone in your family. . . maybe even in your own marriage relationship. You show love. It makes you vulnerable. It risks rejection. It risks hurt. But it is the love that overcomes the world. Jesus set the example by His loving us even from the cross. That kind of love is what He asks of us.

One of the most poignant stories I ever heard was of a woman who had rescued a child from a burning hut. Thatch roofs and open cooking fires often result in tragedy. As her neighbors' hut was burning, this woman rushed in to try to save the people inside. She was only able to get out an infant before the burning roof collapsed on the family. She raised the boy as her own child until he was the age to be able to herd goats and do chores. Then some extended family members came from another village to claim the child. It was going to be up to the chief to make the decision. On the day of the meeting the whole village turned out to listen. The family members made long speeches about how they should have a right to the child. When it came time for the old woman to speak, she stood up but she didn't say a word. She just held up her hands. . . hands that were gnarled and scarred, fingers grown together with webs of scar tissue from the injuries of the fire. The woman, the only mother the boy had ever known, simply stood there with tears on her cheeks and her ugly scarred hands held up for all to see. The chief immediately awarded the boy to the woman who had saved him. The world is looking at the church to see if we have any scars from our service or our sacrifice. They don't want to hear judgment, they want to see love. They want to see if we just talk the talk or if we walk the walk. They want to see if our faith is real and if we are willing to go the distance. The world is watching and waiting. They want to see our hands.

The amazing thing is that the Holy Spirit will do it if we just let go and let Him have His way.

> But you shall receive power when the Holy Spirit has come upon you; and you shall be witnesses to Me in Jerusalem, and in all Judea and Samaria, and to the end of the earth. (Acts 1:8)

> For to this you were called, because Christ also suffered for us, leaving us an example, that you should follow in His steps. (I Peter 2:21)

Pastor Andrew's house in the heart of Pokot Land and *Big Red*, our faithful
Toyota Land Cruiser that never once stranded us in the desert.

The first boys to attend school, in Pastor Andrew's little tin school building.

The school boys were excited to receive a simple thing like a new blanket. David Lotuu, on the ground, was a polio victim we later took to Nairobi for surgery to straighten his legs so he could walk with crutches. He became a strong leader in the church and a music and choir leader.

# Chapter 5

# Night of the Lions

Be sober, be vigilant, because your adversary the devil
walks about like a roaring lion, seeking whom he may
devour.
I Peter 5:8

When you are new on the mission field, you really think you know a lot. As time goes by you find out that you don't know much. One of the projects we took on early in our missionary life was recovering an old Land Rover after Pastor George Kendagor's vehicle had been swept away and buried in the sand when he was trying to cross the flooded Kanyangerang River. The Land Rover was buried nose down in the now-dry river bed. It was a challenge for Dick and son Rick, a couple of mechanics who thought they could fix anything. . .and eventually they did.

On this night we had camped alongside the river bed with about a dozen African volunteers who would help with the shoveling to unearth the Land Rover. The journey had been hot and long and we were all tired and looking forward to a night's sleep. We pitched our tent alongside the road about 100 yards from the river bed. The Kenyans (who did not have a tent) bedded down in the dry river bed in the soft sand. They built a fire and settled in around the fire. I wondered why in that heat anyone would build a fire. It was so very hot that I moved my cot to the door of the tent and slept with my head out the door where there was just a hint of breeze. I drifted off to sleep hearing the pleasant voices of the men in the river bed talking, sometimes singing. It was a peaceful African scene.

Somewhere in the middle of the night the peace was shattered by shrieking sounds in the tree tops. At first I didn't know what was happening. Then I realized it was the baboons who are usually asleep at night. I woke Dick up. "Something is going on out there." "Be quiet and go to sleep," was the reply I got. I lay still and listened. Something was definitely going on. The baboons were not about to "be quiet and go to sleep." I woke Dick again and got the same response. Then I saw that the men in the riverbed had piled brush on their fire and the flames were shooting up into the night sky. I whispered to Dick again but he was very sound asleep. I lay listening, not knowing what was happening or what I should be doing about it. I was, after all, a worrier! Eventually the baboons settled down, the voices in the river bed died down again and I drifted back to sleep.

The next morning we saw what the middle of the night activity was all about. Between our tent and the river bed were the huge tracks of a pride of lions who had passed through during the night. I thought about my head sticking out of the tent … no fire … no gun… no where to run. It was only one of many incidents where God's protection covered our naïveté.

We learned some things that night… being aware of our surroundings… paying attention to warning signs. . .not letting physical tiredness over rule common sense. . .paying attention to the baboons, who obviously had more sense than we had. Pastor Andrew, who lived on the border of the tribal area, told us that when the Turkana cattle raiders came at night the local baboons would scream warnings. Andrew's family learned to listen to the warnings of their furry neighbors.

The Bible says that Satan is like a roaring lion. I Peter 5:8 says: "Be vigilant, because your adversary the devil walks about like a roaring lion, seeking whom he may devour." We hear the roaring of the lion in our culture today. It is in the things we see on television that make us cringe, the things that are being taught to our children in the school system about no clear rules of right and wrong, everything dependant on the circumstance and the belief system of the individual. If we listen, the roaring is all around us. The warning signs are there. (We may even hear a few baboon screams now and then.) But we peacefully slumber off to sleep. Our bellies are full, we are tired from all the activities of our lives, and we don't see the real danger because of the darkness around us. The Africans had it right … build up the fire. That fire that will keep the devil at bay …. the Holy Spirit in our lives …. our gathering together for worship and for Bible Study to keep the things of God burning brightly in our lives … speaking up for the morals and standards that God has given us… standards that are set in stone – not negotiable – not situational – not bendable. God's Word is a plumb bob by which we can rightly measure our lives and our activities and our standards.

We were lucky that night along the river bed. We could very well have been killed because of our lack of vigilance. We need to wake up and to recognize the signs.

Lions are not about roaring; that is only what we hear. Lions are about devouring. And we can be sure that Satan is about devouring. The Scripture makes it very clear. Ephesians 6:12 says, "... we do not wrestle against flesh and blood, but against principalities, against powers, against the rulers of darkness of this age, against spiritual hosts of wickedness in high places." Jesus said to Peter in Luke 22:31, "Satan has asked for you that he may sift you as wheat." We need the fire, the heaping on of the fuel so that the fire stays bright enough to keep Satan at bay. We need the light of Jesus Christ. We need to fuel it daily in our lives, to keep it burning and bright, to stay within its light and warmth, to treasure Christian friends, Christian music, and to keep our talk and our walk Christ-like. Christ has already overcome and has given us the power to overcome in our lives. Revelation 12:11 tells us that the martyrs *overcame* by the blood of the Lamb: "They overcame ... by the blood of the Lamb and by the word of their testimony."

Post note: Oh yeah, the Land Rover that was the purpose of this exercise. Dick and Rick spent months removing every grain of sand from gauges, etc, welding the frame and rebuilding it from the ground up. It served Pastor George for many years as he took the gospel across the hills and valleys of Western Kenya.

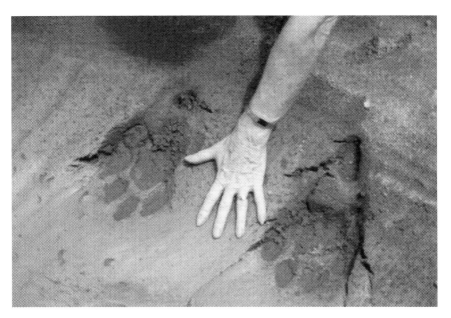

Lion prints in the sand.

Pastor George's Land Rover buried in the sand after being overtaken
by the flooded Kanyangerang River during heavy rains.

Pastor George, Dick and volunteers digging out the Land
Rover, to begin the rebuilding and restoration process.

Dick, returning the keys to Pastor George – a renovated Land
Rover ready for the Lord's service, taking the gospel across
the hills and valleys of West Pokot for many years.

# Chapter 6

## Poured Out

We glory in our tribulations, knowing that tribulation
produces perseverance . . .and hope does not disappoint,
because the love of God has been poured out in our hearts
through the Holy Spirit who was given to us.
Romans 5:3,5

Ruth Hover was my spiritual mother. Her beautiful Christian life impacted me as I was growing up, as it had many other young lives shaped for Christian service by her teaching and example. She was at the airport to see us off, but even as we were en route to Kenya we learned that she had been killed in an auto accident. I was not to see her on this earth again. At summer Bible camp Ruth was one who had stood at the bonfire and gave wonderful devotionals that stirred your heart and made you want to do *something* for the Lord, even if you weren't quite sure what. One story that Ruth told at bonfire was the story of David's drink offering sacrifice. How did that story come into my mind twenty years later at one of my lowest moments? Only the promise of the Holy Spirit's comfort can answer that question. God is so faithful.

In the early years we did safari ministry, kind of like camping trips, packing up our supplies and descending down the winding road that was cut out of the side of the escarpment wall, into the Great Rift Valley floor. The thousands of people who lived there had never heard the name of Jesus. They lived in little mud huts, sustained by their herds of cattle and goats, and followed a nomadic lifestyle of searching for water and graze for their animals. We would set up camp and try to make contact with the people to begin to earn their trust and be able to tell them about Jesus. When our supplies ran out and we were totally "bushy" we would head back up the escarpment to resupply, take a bath, work on equipment and set out again on safari. This nomadic life style lasted several years until we established a base camp out in the valley

It was on one of our returns to the base in Kitale town that we came home to find our house totally ransacked and looted by thieves. It was devastating to realize that the things that we had carefully selected and packed into barrels on the other side of the world to set up a home in Africa were gone. So many little things that held such memories for me were just gone. My purse which I had left behind so nothing would happen to it in the bush held treasured photos of my kids (pictures that would probably end up discarded in a ditch somewhere) and a watch my mom had given me on my 18th birthday that had such special meaning for me. All were gone. Everything in the house was dumped out and overturned and about two feet of debris covered the floors. I was so overcome with anger and despair sitting in the middle of the rubble that had been our house that I didn't know how I could go on. Then from somewhere in the depths of my soul and memory came Auntie Ruth's story of David and his drink offering. How powerfully the Holy Spirit ministers to us in our darkest moments.

DAVID... was hiding in the dry heat of the desert, thirsting for the water from his home well. Now this is a story missionaries can relate to. . . our missing the Burger King or our favorite Chinese food and sitting around talking about it; drinking lukewarm water and dreaming of ice cubes clinking in the glass. Yes, we could relate to David longing for the cool water from his well at home.

Ruth's bonfire message had related how David's band of mighty men, out of their love for David, risked their lives to go through the enemy lines to bring David the water from his well. David was so touched and moved by what his men had done for him that he could not bring himself to drink it. Do you know what David did with that water? It was so precious to him that he poured it out as a sacrifice to the Lord. As I sat there in the midst of the rubble of what had been my house, the memory of Ruth's message from the Lord ministered deeply to my angry, troubled heart. I began to mentally picture the things I'd lost being poured out as a sacrifice, one by one: my watch, the photos of my kids, our household items and the little things that I treasured. I pictured them being poured out unto the Lord, not taken from me by a gang of thugs, but given up as a sacrifice to God. An indescribable peace came over me as one by one I released those things.

After that, every time we were robbed, and it happened often, I went through that *poured out like* a *drink offering* exercise. Those things were not taken from me; I poured them out. It helped me to put material things into perspective. This exercise of *pouring out* helped when we faced the darkest time still to come. When we lost our friend Lyle in a terrible jail experience, we tried to think of him as being poured out for God and not taken away by the actions of a paranoid government. Yes, even in the darkest hours God sends His comfort, His message, His love to lift us up, His everlasting arms to sustain us.

> But those who wait on the Lord shall renew their strength; they shall mount up with wings like eagles; They shall run and not be weary; They shall walk and not faint. (Isaiah 40:31)

*Let It Go!*

I was often teased about my protective attitude towards my stash of Tupperware. One of the churches had given me a Tupperware shower before we left for Kenya and I treasured every piece that kept things clean and bug free in the bush. I would have a major tizzy if one of the lids went missing. I finally realized you can be just as covetous over a barrel full of Tupperware as anyone can be over a big bank account. It was one of the things I finally had to make peace with and just let it go. I have a magnet on my refrigerator today that says: *"The most important things in life are not things."* How we cling to our things. We covet them. We clutch them. We worry about them. We struggle to maintain them. But they are ONLY THINGS.

In parts of Africa they trap monkeys by putting nuts in a narrow mouth jar and fastening the jar down. The monkeys will reach into the jar and grab the nuts, but then their fist can't fit through the narrow mouth of the jar. Even as their captors seize them and they scream in terror, they will not let go of the nuts in order to make their escape. We are so like that with our things. We can't release them, even for God, even for freedom. We spend our lives for our things. We work and worry and slave. It's been said that we don't really own things, but that our things own us. Things are not evil of themselves. Money is not evil. The Bible says that it is the *love* of money that is evil. It is our blind quest for the things that we think will make us happy and they never do. I can remember being on my way home from the mall with the price tag still on the dress and I'm already thinking about the shoes I want to go with it. The first payment isn't made on the truck and we are already thinking about the boat we want behind it.

The satisfaction we get from things is so fleeting. It never truly satisfies us. I was always puzzled by the bankers who threw themselves off their bank buildings when the stock market crashed. Was life so cheap that they could not go on without their wealth? Why not just go build a cabin and raise chickens? And live.

We keep hanging on. We live in a youth culture where everyone is desperately trying to hang on to their youth. If we watch the ads, it's everywhere; but it's a losing battle. We hang on to lost relationships and bitterness over hurts. We hang on. Whatever holds us captive, we've got to let it go. Unclench our fist and let it go. "The lilies of the field they toil not," but God takes care of them. (Matthew 6:28 KJV)

I cling to Revelation 12:11 that says the martyrs *overcame* because "they did not love their lives to the death." They "overcame." They were not victims. They were over-comers. We don't know what is coming in the future. We live in uncertain times. We **do** know we can be over-comers if we remember that we are eternal beings … just passing through. We sing, "*This world is not my home, I'm just passing through,*" and, "*Turn your eyes upon Jesus, look full in His wonderful face, and the things of earth will grow strangely dim in the light of His glory and grace.*"

We sing it but do we believe it?

> For all that is in the world—the lust of the flesh, the lust of the eyes, and the pride of life—is not of the Father but of the world. And the world is passing away, and the lust of it, but he who does the will of God abides forever (I John 2:16-17)

# Chapter 7

---

# The Early Years . . .
# Boots on the Ground

Pure and undefiled religion before God our Father is this:
to visit orphans and widows in their trouble, and to keep
oneself unspotted from the world.
James 1:27

Oh, those early years! They were the hardest and they were the best. We were such an oddity, we funny white-skinned people. Kids would run, babies would cry and whole herds of cows would stop and stare. The people gave Dick the nick-name, "the man with hair like a cow's tail." (In Pokot that was a compliment.) The Northern Frontier District of Pokot was a closed area until some years after Kenya's 1963 Independence. It was closed and culturally protected, so North Pokot was pretty much caught in a time warp. We were the first white people to go in after the government opened the area. Most of the Pokot people in that area had never seen anyone white. After the children got over being afraid, they would sidle up to Dick to feel the red hair on his arms or run their fingers through my funny blonde hair. If I tried to find some privacy to take a *bush break*, there would be all these little faces peeking around the bushes to see if I was really white all over. The kids would later tell us that they thought our skin would be squishy to touch.

On one of our early safari trips into the bush I noticed a baby with an ugly sore and dug out my tube of A & D ointment. Immediately a line formed of mamas and babies with skin sores. The line quickly turned into a crowd pressing me against the mud wall of a hut and I was trapped there treating skin problems until my ointment and my endurance were gone. I fled back to the car surrounded by mothers begging for help for their babies.

We needed to do something, but what? Dick had first aid training from his police force days and my mom was a nurse, but we were far from qualified for this. We appealed to Dr. Bob who worked with the neighboring Turkana tribe and he set us up with a little medical box and instructions for treating the simple things. Dick became adept at treating the tropical skin ulcers, caused by the ever-present thorns. The sores could go clear to the bone and be quite serious. A little trimming of the crust with the good old Swiss Army Knife and applying a little medicine could work wonders. We always carried hydrogen peroxide, antibiotic ointment and a big jug of gentian violet that worked miracles on the many skin infections, scabies, etc.

As we traveled up and down the road the word would go out. We called it the "bush telegraph" and we never figured out how the word would travel through the bush faster than our car traveled the road. If we left early in the morning we would find people already gathered all along the road waiting for medicine. We quickly learned to identify the ever-present malaria and would have everyone with symptoms form a line for malaria medicine. Then we learned another valuable use for gentian violet. We needed to keep people who had already received medicine from going to the back of the line to get a second dose of pills. A simple X of the bright purple gentian violet, on the forehead of those already treated, sorted them out. There were such miracles of modern medicine for people who had not had antibiotics. A fifty cent tube of tetracycline could stop the dreaded trachoma that caused blindness. Imagine being able to save someone's sight with fifty cents worth of medicine. Life in the thorn bush is hard enough when you can see.

During the years before we were able to build a proper clinic at Kiwawa, we carried the little medical box everywhere we went. Often our *Big Red* Toyota Land Cruiser served as an ambulance to haul people the one hundred miles to the nearest hospital. There is little hope for a breech birth delivery in the bush. Dispensing medicine from *Big Red* was a challenge as people crowded in so tight around the car. I would often stand up on the tail gate to get above the mêlée, the heat of the pressing crowd and the ever-present flies. The women adorned their tightly twisted strands of hair with cow fat and mica which was very attractive sparkling in the sun, but was always accompanied by a cloud of flies. As I would stand on the tailgate dozens of little black hands would be touching my legs followed by giggles and squeals and then big smiles on little faces if I looked in their direction. Of course I began to carry bags of hard candy which just increased the kid following.

It was the best of times. It was the simple life. There is no place more comfortable than being in the center of God's will. Bumping up and down those horrendous roads with the flies and the heat and knowing we were exactly where God wanted us to be; falling into bed at night exhausted and totally, totally happy was truly the good life. We still remember those days most fondly.

> I will both lie down in peace and sleep; for you alone, O
> Lord, make me dwell in safety . (Psalm 4:8)

People lined up waiting for medicine. The "bush telegraph" somehow always reached the people who needed help and brought them to wait along the road for the vehicle to pass.

A typical Pokot family waits along the road.

The fashion statement for Pokot women, tightly wound strands
of hair rolled with cow fat and dusted with mica; a beautiful
sparkly attraction always accompanied by clouds of flies.

A fifty-cent tube of tetracycline saves the eye sight of people
infected with dreaded trachoma, a disease carried by the flies.

Scabies results from lack of water to wash. Legs covered
with scabies infection left this little girl unable to walk.
Her mama carried her many miles for treatment.

Simple antibiotics can work miracles and malaria medicine
saves many lives, especially the children.

Jane Hamilton

Our first house in Pokot (on right), made of sticks and mud with a tin roof. Pastor John Mosonik's house on the left.

The first church building at Kiwawa was a thatched roof shade shelter, protecting from the harsh sun in the dry season and from heavy rains during the three month wet season.

# Chapter 8

# Warriors on the Mountain

> ...for you were slain, and have redeemed us to God by
> your blood out of every tribe and tongue and people and
> nation.
> Revelation 5:9b

I huddled there in the front seat of the Land Cruiser, knowing the video camera was on the back seat but I was afraid to show myself by climbing over to retrieve it. And once I got it, would I have the courage to film what I was seeing play out in front of me? It was not a place for women and I knew it. As badly as I wanted to capture the scene on film, I held my place and watched in awe.

There sat Dick on a log next to the District Commissioner, Honorable Francis Lotodo, with streams of Pokot warriors coming down off the mountain to meet with their leader. Hundreds of warriors came in serpentine down the steep paths, feet pounding the ground, spears brandished above their heads; their deep undulating chants almost shaking the earth beneath them. Each one stopped in front of the log to pay homage to Commissioner Lotodo, with a noble genuflect, one knee to the ground, and a dip of the spear, as they filed by. Many of them glared at the white stranger, not knowing who he was or why he was there. Francis Lotodo was a friend and had invited Dick to this meeting to give his endorsement for the work we were entering into with the Pokot tribe, one of the wildest, most resistant people groups in Kenya.

Over a thousand warriors fanned out on the ground in front of the two men on the log. A thousand warrior voices, deep-throated guttural chants, alive with passion and zeal, echoing off the hills, sent chills down my spine. I watched in awe of the pageantry of this gathering of warriors who came to pay homage to a political leader of the Kenya government, but one who was also their accepted tribal leader, having risen to heights through their own ranks. This fierce allegiance from one of the most combatant warrior tribes in Kenya would later bring on government fear and suspicion that led to harrowing times for Lotodo, but he emerged strong politically, later becoming a Member of Parliament. He is remembered by many as the "King of Pokot." On this day there was no doubt the place of honor that Francis Polisi Lotodo held with the Pokot men. For Dick, it was a memorable experience that he treasured and was grateful to be a part of. For me, I always regretted not having the courage to capture it on film.

On another occasion Dick stood in a clearing with Timothy Lopongo, the chief who granted us the land for the Kiwawa Mission. A large herd of cattle were gathered together in the clearing as a big bull was led around the herd. It was the scene of a sacrifice to protect the cattle from an impending raid. Chief Timothy offered the spear to Dick to do the honors but he had the presence of mind to decline. After ceremonial rituals were completed, Chief Timothy walked up to the bull and with a short flick of the wrist speared the animal and it immediately fell dead. When they cut it open Dick was amazed to see that the top of the heart had been cut with that almost imperceptible thrust of the spear, so expertly executed.

That experience made it all the more impressive when we later watched a group of young warriors playing war games. They would run up behind and tag another warrior with a stick carefully thrust at the heart location. In real warfare, the hand-to-hand combat depended on the quickness and skill of the spear thrusts. Each warrior carried two spears, one to throw and one to do close-up battle. Their shields were made of thick leather from elephant or cape buffalo hide, sometimes metal, with a crafted handle of leather on the back side. These shields could be used to deflect the enemy spears as they did close-up combat. The shields were plain, the only adornment an occasional ostrich feather ball or a rare shell casing from a gun. The traditions of warfare and the skill of the warriors in handling shield and spear all went away later when guns were introduced and the fighting took on new and deadlier engagements. Eventually the steady influence of the gospel and the church would turn the hearts of the young men away from bloodshed and to the Prince of Peace, Jesus.

A warrior demonstrates the use of spear and shield in close combat.

Jane Hamilton

The men's hats were often made with hair of their fathers and grandfathers, adorned with colorful mud and ostrich feathers.

Lip plugs of wood, metal or ivory pierced under the lower lip.

# Chapter 9

# The Bridge . . Blood Sacrifice

> But in those sacrifices there is a reminder of sins every
> year. For it is not possible that the blood of bulls and goats
> could take away sins.
> Heb 10:3-4

How do you reach across the time gap of generations to a people locked in a centuries-old culture of cattle raiding and animistic tribal rituals and begin to explain to them a God of love and forgiveness? The Pokot god Tororot, in their belief system, is a god distant and unreachable who sends sickness to punish and famine to chastise.

The Pokot are a warrior culture and have for centuries carried on tribal fighting with neighboring tribes over the cattle around which their lives revolve. A young man cannot marry until he has captured enough cows to pay her father the bride price. When the dry season comes, a family will only survive if they have enough cattle to provide the life-giving milk and blood drink that sustains them through the hard times. They rotate bleeding the cattle with a stubby tipped arrow that penetrates but does not damage the livestock. That protein-rich blood mixed with milk provides a drink that sustains the family through the difficult dry season. The Pokot believe that god intended for them to have all the cattle. Unfortunately, the neighboring Karamojong and Turkana tribes believe the same thing. So warfare over the cattle has gone on for generations, taking the lives of many young men.

As we began to provide water wells and medical help, we were welcomed in the villages and sometimes invited to traditional ceremonies and celebrations. From this interaction with the tribe we accidentally discovered *the bridge*. That bridge was the issue of blood sacrifice.

We learned that when a Pokot warrior kills an enemy in battle he must go through a purification rite. A pure white unspotted goat is chosen for a sacrifice. Then the white strips of goat skin are tied to the arms, knees and calves and worn for a period of seclusion while the young man stays in the bush away from his family.

In learning about this rite we had discovered a bridge from their culture which helped us to explain and helped them to understand, the perfect spotless sacrificial lamb, Jesus Christ, slain for our purification and cleansing. It was a concept from their own culture to help them understand the sacrifice of Jesus. We remembered reading a book years earlier about "eternity in their hearts" that said that every culture has bridges that can be used to explain the gospel. This ages-old Pokot ritual of the white spotless goat was the picture parable to begin to teach about a loving God who willingly sent his son into the world to search us out and to become our sacrificial lamb; not a far-away god who sent punishment but a God who loves us and reaches out for us and makes us His own children. Thousands of Pokot have now understood and have claimed Jesus' sacrifice as their own. For the Christians there are no more appeasements to angry gods for the sickness of their children; no more fear of displeasing a god that they did not understand; no more darkness. Now they have the perfect light of Jesus Christ freeing them from centuries of fear and superstition.

> In this is love, not that we loved God, but that He loved us and sent His Son to be an atoning sacrifice for our sins. (John 4:10)

> We have been made holy through the sacrifice of the body of Jesus Christ once for all. (Hebrews 10:10)

> My little children, these things I write to you, so that you may not sin. And if any one sins, we have an advocate with the Father, Jesus Christ, the Righteous. And He himself is the propitiation for our sins, and not for ours only but also for the whole world. (I John 2:1-2)

> But now . . . He has appeared to put away sin by the sacrifice of Himself. (Hebrews 9:26b)

"Their Blood is Crying from the Ground":

As Jesus began to work in the hearts and lives of Pokot men, gradually they turned away from cattle raiding. On one occasion a group of several thousand armed warriors, from Karamoja in Uganda and the Pokot from Kenya, came together for a peace meeting along the border. It was a historic day for that many armed warriors to be together without bloodshed. One wrong move or one fired shot could have let to a terrible slaughter. But the groups sat soberly and listened as they heard pastors from both tribes beg for peace. One pastor told the story of Cain and Abel and how the blood of the slain brother cried out from the ground. "Your brothers' blood is crying from the ground" the pastor said. He asked: "How many of you have lost brothers to raiding?" Many hands were raised. *Their blood is crying from the ground,"* the pastor told them. It was a powerful meeting, the first of many that would begin to change the warring lifestyle, as the message of Jesus began to change hearts on both sides of the border.

When a young man kills an enemy in battle, one side of his
body is scarred with arrow cuts rubbed with ashes, forming a
finely tooled pattern that is a life-long symbol of bravery.

Warriors preparing for a dance; two on the right have the strips
of white goat skin from a sacrifice for a kill in battle.

The tribal elders make the decisions about the cattle
raids and plan the strategy for attacks.

Jane Hamilton

# Chapter 10

# Water of Life – Opening the Door for the Gospel

They shall neither hunger nor thirst, neither heat nor sun
shall strike them; for He who has mercy on them shall
lead them, even by the springs of water He will guide
them.
Isaiah 49:10

The turning point was the water. It was the water that opened the door to the hearts of the Pokot. It was the water that brought the illusive men out of the cover of the bush to interact with the strange white *mzungu* (foreigner) and ultimately to open their hearts to the gospel. It was the water that made possible the schools, clinics, churches and permanent villages that grew up around the wells.

Growing up in the Pacific Northwest, water wasn't really a precious thing. In fact, sometimes it was downright annoying. It fell endlessly from the sky at the most inopportune times, when we longed for those beautiful days of sunshine when we could be out and about . . .without an umbrella.

Finding myself in the dry Northern Pokot District of Kenya, I learned just how precious water really is. I learned by hauling jerry cans of drinking water from 100 miles away. I learned by searching for it in the desert, boiling it, straining it, sometimes drinking the brown lukewarm water and being glad to have any water at all. I learned how precious water is by watching the women dig by hand and primitive tools, into the dry river beds, deeper and deeper as the dry season went on, just to get the scarce brown water for livestock and families. Sometimes the hand-dug pit wells would be six women deep, with women hoisting the wooden basins of water hand over hand up to the top. There was always the danger of cave-ins or a thirsty cow falling in on top of them. More than once Dick had to use the winch on the Toyota to pull a cow out of a hand dug pit well.

Little girls walked for miles to carry a jug of water that would be the family's ration for one day. Imagine caring for your family on one jerry can of water a day. Pokot families live on a daily ration of the water that we use in one bath or one flush of the toilet.

We never got used to seeing the deep tropical skin ulcers and the dreaded trachoma eye disease from not having enough water to wash. Trachoma is carried by flies. It causes eye lashes to turn under, scratching the eye, eventually resulting in blindness. It was common to see a blind grandma holding one end of a long stick with a child holding the other end, leading the grandmother around the village, up and down the hills and gullies. That was the little girl's childhood, being grandma's eyes, all because there was no water to wash.

How often I would see a mother in the bush take a swig of water in her mouth from her precious little gourd of water and then spit-spray the child's face and hands with a little shower of water trying to clean the child. So many children suffered with scabies and skin sores from not having water to wash. All this suffering was from the lack of a simple thing like water.

The British had drilled wells during colonial times but almost all were broken. Dick had not gone to Africa to do a water ministry but there it was. It was a need we could not ignore and God had equipped Dick to fix things. He was just a farm boy with a knack for making things work and God had taken him exactly where He needed a guy with a wrench. As Dick began to fix the wells, the men who had been aloof to the white strangers began to come and interact with us. They told Dick: "We see you love us because you love our cows." The repairing of wells opened the door into the lives of the people. The physical water allowed us to bring them to the living water, Jesus Christ. It was showing God's love in a tangible way and it touched the hearts of the people.

It was always a thrill seeing the joy and celebration when a well was repaired or a new well was drilled. Children laughed and washed with all the excitement of a Christmas morning. One old man laughed and said: "Listen, even the birds are happy to have water." We built water troughs at the pumps for the cattle, only to find that women would walk long distances and chase the cows away to bathe their children in the water troughs. There was no other way in the desert to give a child a simple thing like a bath. Abundant fresh water was like a miracle for the mamas of Pokot land.

As we traveled around fixing the wells, we often camped out at the well site. It gave us a unique opportunity to interact with the people on their own turf. As I cooked our meals there was always an audience. I would see men later with rings made out of my silverware. Little silver rings with Oneida patterns adorning rough, tough warrior hands! One unusual ring was made from a fork with the prongs sticking up. He actually ate with it! It always made me smile that we wanted their carved artifacts and they wanted our silverware.

We abandoned our tent living early on because the tent was just a trap for flies and heat. The inside roof of the tent would literally be covered with flies. Rick spent a lot of time with a fly swatter, keeping count of the hundreds of flies, trying to best his record. For a teenage boy, sport is where you find it. In lieu of the tent, we slept on the roof rack of the Toyota. The wooden roof rack was much more comfortable, even knowing it was a quick hop for a lion and a natural height for the deadly mamba snakes who hung out in the thorn trees, but *oh*, the fresh air, the beauty of the stars in the clear pristine night sky of the bush of Africa, and the vast stillness and silence of the desert, were beyond wonderful.

Gospel Recordings had put out Bible cassette tapes in the Pokot language complete with picture boards. I could always draw a crowd of women and kids to sit and listen to the tapes. Later when we had trained young Pokot evangelists, they would go out with us to preach to the people and answer questions. As Dick would work on the wells, a crowd of men would always gather to watch. They were exposed to the love of Jesus in a very real practical way being demonstrated in the well repairs. We always prayed before the work began and a prayer of thanksgiving after the beautiful life-giving water would begin to flow. One man said, "We walk miles to carry water and we didn't know it was right under our feet." Once a village head man told us that he had seen the Christian women meeting under the tree to pray for water and he had ridiculed them, but, he said, "I can see that their God is real and has answered their prayers." The water was always a message of the love of God and of Jesus, the Water of Life.

At one place Dick was getting ready to repair a well, and as he pulled the old pipes out of the well, they were full of rusty water. An old woman standing there with her jug was carefully catching every bit of the water as it drained out of the pipes. When Dick got the pump out of the well he realized he had not brought along water to wash the parts. It was an hour drive back to Kiwawa so he asked the old woman for some of her water. She got up and raced off with her jug. The men standing around grabbed her and brought her back telling her to give Dick the water to clean the pump. She refused. Dick explained to her that if she would give him some of her old rusty water that in just a little while there would be plenty of clean fresh water for everyone. After a long, loud, animated discussion, the village men finally prevailed and drug her back where she begrudgingly gave Dick half of her water. When the well was fixed and the fresh water started flowing, she poured her old water out on the ground and filled her jug with clean fresh water. How like us with God, we thought. He gives us and then asks for some of it back and we stubbornly hang on to it. When, like the old woman, if we will give some back, He will supply our needs abundantly.

We saw such changes in lifestyle where there were pumping wells. The tropical skin ulcers and eye diseases disappeared in areas where there was fresh well water. Schools and clinics were established for the families. The normally nomadic Pokot settled into permanent villages where the old and the little ones could stay in one place when the adults went with the cattle in search of grazing.

As we saw the transformation of lives because of the water, we gained a new appreciation for the Scriptures' words about the *Water of Life*: satisfaction for the thirsty soul; refreshing of days; cleanliness; life-giving pure, wonderful sustaining water. Water makes all things possible. Without it there can be no life. How true that is in both the physical and the spiritual realms. How desperately we need the Water of Life for our thirsty souls. Jesus is the Water of life. Yes, the Pokot understood that one, far better than we Westerners who often take water so for granted. Precious water of life.

> But whoever drinks of the water that I shall give him will never thirst. But the water that I shall give him shall become in him a fountain of water springing up into everlasting life. (John 4:14)

Then the angel showed me the river of the water of life, as clear as crystal, flowing from the throne of God and of the Lamb. (Rev 22:1)

For the Lamb who is in the midst of the throne will shepherd them and lead them to living fountains of waters. And God will wipe away every tear from their eyes. (Rev 7:17)

Women dig deep into the dry river beds for the precious
little water that sustains life during the dry season.

Dangers are cave-ins or a thirsty cow falling into the well.
These hand-dug wells can be four to six women deep.

Jane Hamilton

The scarce brown water is rationed out for family
use and for watering the livestock.

A young girl leads her blind grandmother through the bush, the
result of trachoma eye disease from no water to wash.

The beginning of the water ministry was the repairing of the old wells that had been put in during British colonial rule. This provision of water opened the door for the preaching of the gospel of the Water of Life, Jesus.

Repairing one of the old wells that had been drilled by the British. It always drew a crowd of men for gospel outreach.

Drilling equipment provided by World Vision for the drilling
of over 150 wells, providing life-giving water.

The drilling of wells has made possible the establishment of schools,
clinics and permanent villages for the nomadic Pokot.

The children feel the pure joy of clean fresh water.

Jane Hamilton

A watering trough built for cattle becomes a bath tub for Pokot
babies who have no other way to bathe in the desert

Girls head home with the family's daily supply of water. The trip
is often a several mile walk to deliver the precious cargo.

A mother washes her child's hands with one precious
mouth-full of water, so scarce in the desert.

The endless job of repairing the pumps that are busy 24 hours
a day during the dry season, with herds of cattle and goats
lined up waiting their turn. Water is life in the desert.

Jane Hamilton

Teaching the young Pokot men to do the repairs on the pumps.

A camel waits patiently for the last bolt to be in place.

The children are always the first to try the pump after repairs.
Simple things like washing are a luxury in the desert.

Clean hands and a big thank you for a repaired well.

A welcome at the village of Kases in 2003 turned into a challenge for our hearts:

An old woman stood to speak, one of many welcoming us on a bright warm day in the little village of Kases. We had just returned from furlough and were visiting the village churches. The old mama began her greeting, like the others, talking about the things we had done in the years we had worked in Kenya, feel-good words that always accompanied the welcomes. Then her face changed from talking about good things and she started a story that cut into our hearts. During the very dry time of the year in 1997 the whole village had been forced to move across the border into Uganda near to a river where they could get water for their families and cattle. One day while the men were out with the cows looking for grazing, the Karamajong raiders came. They killed 57 people, many women but most of them children who could not run fast enough to get away or hide. Then the old woman lifted her beaded necklace to show us where she, herself, had been shot in the shoulder. "It was because we didn't have any water," she said. She pointed her finger at Dick for a moment and then she sat down. The silence that followed her words overpowered us. Dick made a promise on that day that we would come back and drill a well for them. One more very poignant reminder of the difference a village well can make in the lives of the people. Today there is an active church and a big primary school at Kases, made possible because of the drilling of the water well.

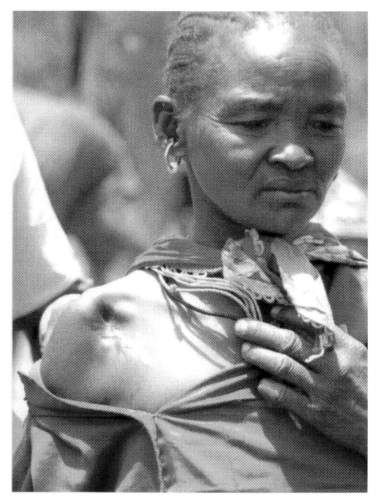

The woman whose plea brought the promise of water for her village, showing where she was shot when fifty seven women and children from her village were killed by raiders as they searched for water in Uganda. "It was all because of water," she said. Today a drilled well provides that precious water for church, school and community.

# Chapter 11

## Children of the Desert

Jesus said, "Let the little children come to Me . . . for of
such are the Kingdom of Heaven."
Matthew 19:14

Six out of ten Kara Pokot babies died before they could walk when we first arrived on the scene. Imagine giving birth to ten children and only four of them surviving long enough to become toddlers. The Pokot people love and treasure their children, but it is a rugged land that takes a terrible toll on the little ones. The children, a natural resource and hope for the future of the tribe, are raised with love, discipline and a strong sense of responsibility. Young girls are tasked with fetching water for the family and it is common to see a girl as young as six with a baby on her back that is her responsibility for the day. The bride price of cattle for marriageable daughters will increase the family's herds and wealth. Sons are necessary for the herding and care of the cattle and goats. The wealthier a man, the more sons he needs to take care of the animals. Boys from about six years old are sent out with small herds of goats and young cattle to graze. As the boys grow older they take full responsibility for finding water and grazing for large herds and protecting them from cattle raiders and wild animals. We didn't see juvenile delinquency in Pokot culture because teens were an integral and valued part of the family and society, who fully understood their roles and responsibilities.

Pokot children learn work and responsibility at an early age.

The children are raised with love, strict discipline and a strong
sense of self worth. Girls as young as six care for baby siblings.

A potential student checks out the poles that will become the stick
and mud school building at Kiwawa, the first school in the area.

Many schools began under the trees with village children

In 1976, we started the first schools, and for several decades ours were the only schools available for the children of 50,000 Kara Pokot people. In the beginning the chiefs decreed that each family send one boy to school. Some came kicking and screaming as Dad came dragging the naked little boy who had been chosen from that family. Other boys came anxious to learn the "talking papers" that could carry messages.

The chief decreed that one boy from each family would be sent to school. In the early years families did not allow girls in school.

We started with first grade only and then added another grade every year. Sometimes teenage boys would come to first grade wanting to learn to read; big lanky boys with long legs squeezed under the small desks, but eager to learn. Because of the nomadic lifestyle of the Pokot it was necessary to have boarding dormitories for the children. In years of drought, when there was no food at home, the school rolls swelled as children came to school for the daily meals. Eventually the boarding school at Kiwawa had over 600 children. Little minds were opened to the wonders of the outside world and hearts were opened to the message and love of Jesus. Devotions were held nightly and Bible classes were taught in the schools; Bible teachings were approved and promoted by the Kenya government.

During famine times the meals at the school might be
the only food the children would receive.

The Kenya school system follows the British schedule of three month terms with one month break between each term. Every school break we watched little tykes head out into the bush in search of their nomadic families. Could this little first grader find his way for miles through the bush? Of course he could. He was Pokot and this vast bush was his home. Each child had a little tin suitcase to keep personal things under his dorm bunk. Into the tin box went the school uniform (lovingly sewn by church women in America) and out of the box came the *shuka* cloth or an old pair of ragged shorts that would be worn on the trek home. Sometimes a sheet off his bed would serve as the *shuka*, tied across one shoulder and flapping loosely around the body. It was amazing to see the children easily transition from one world to the other. As they went home to their families they carried with them the lessons they learned, the Bible stories and gospel songs. Slowly the message penetrated into the unreached villages and mountains surrounding Kiwawa mission. The next generation of school teachers, nurses, policemen and government officials were being prepared in those first schools to take their places as leaders.

School boys packed their
uniforms into little tin
boxes and donned the
traditional shuka for the
trek out to find their
nomadic families.

The first generation to learn to read and write proved to be good students. Government teachers taught in the national language so children who knew only Pokot had to learn Swahili for first grade and English at third grade.

Families eventually realized there was benefit for the girls to come to school and the gates of learning were opened for them.

Girls were not sent to school in the early days as families saw no value in educating girls who were destined to be wives and mothers. That changed as the value of school was recognized and girls were able to come and learn. But it was always a heart ache when older men would bring bride price cattle to the fathers of the girls and come claim girls from the school to add wife number five or six to an old guy's family. Tearful girls would be forced into marriages they did not want. There are many tragic stories of girls who fell in love with boys at the school and then were dragged off to the life the culture demanded of them. Sometimes the old men would come to the track meets watching the girls compete to see who were the fastest and strongest so they could select their new wives and decide on the bride price. A strong young girl who could gather and weave branches to build a solid mud hut, haul water for the animals and produce strong sons was worth about 20 cows or equivalent of goats, maybe even a couple of camels. It always angered me to see the grizzly old men sizing up the young girls. I wanted to go break up those groups sitting on the hillside, but we knew the cultural changes would have to come as the gospel changed things. Eventually it did. It was a joyful day when we had the first Christian wedding. Benjamin and Mary had fallen in love, gotten her father's permission, and Benjamin's father paid the cows for the bride price so they could marry. They have spent their lives pastoring the church, an example to the community of what a Biblical marriage can be.

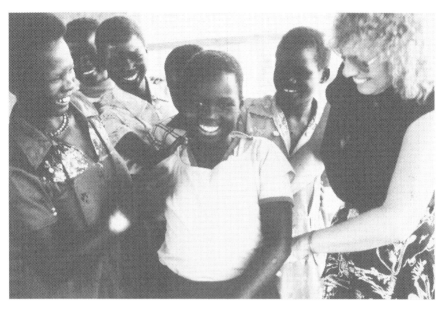

School uniforms, sewn with love by Christian women in USA. Elizabeth and Jane helping to "try on." Always a happy time for the kids.

Eventually the school at Kiwawa numbered over 600 children,
shown here in front of the church in their new school uniforms

Jane Hamilton

*First Pokot to Qualify for Nairobi Boys School*

Kiwawa Primary School produced many top students in the district exams. Two of our boys qualified to be the first Pokot to attend the prestigious Nairobi Boys School, which was once an all-white academy for the children of the British colonials. Joseph and Pius had hardly seen cities and electric lights when we loaded them up for the trip to Nairobi. We purchased the white shirts, blazers and ties needed for the school uniforms, along with soccer togs and required necessities. It was a trip into an unknown life for those two. The cities and the lights along the way and then the capital city of Nairobi opened a whole new world for them.

When we reached the hotel where we would spend the night, Dick went to check us in while I watched the suitcases. When we were ready to go up to our rooms, we started to get on the elevator. "NO!" they protested. No way were they getting in that little room. They had been standing watching and the door would open and people got in but when the door opened again, the people were *gone.* So we ended up toting our luggage up two flights of stairs to our rooms. The jump from the bush of Pokotland to the big city of Nairobi was just too much to take in one day, but they quickly adjusted to city life and enjoyed the advantages of being part of one of the best high schools in Kenya.

Pius and Joseph in their new school blazers entered a new world at
the Nairobi Boys School, the first Pokot students at the school.

Later, as we would drive through Pokot, we were flagged down and
greeted by people in villages and centers all over the area who had been
students at Kiwawa and now were the leaders of the society. The schools have
produced their fruit. Today the government has built and maintains schools
throughout the area, supplying teachers, books and food. The mission still
sponsors many of the schools with dormitories run by the mission, a great
tool for reaching the hearts and minds of the young Pokot students. All the
years of schooling and Bible teaching have changed a generation of Pokot
and turned on a light reaching into an entire culture.

# Chapter 12

# Elizabeth

*You O Lord, are a shield for me; my glory and the one
who lifts up my head
Psalms 3:3*

We heard the rhythmic pounding of the bells early in the morning, as the men came closer and closer. At first, when we had heard the high-pitched warbling of the women, we all stopped to hear if it was warning of enemy raiders coming. Then we heard the ankle bells and we knew it was Pokot men celebrating. The ankle bells are worn by the men for special occasions, a dance or a marriage celebration, a clan get together, or perhaps some young men going through manhood rituals. When a large group of men run in serpentine through the bush wearing the ankle bells, they can be heard for a great distance, their chimes echoing through the valleys and bouncing off the hills.

Not like the treks when the warriors move silently on their way to a raid, naked except for a black *shuka* (cloth) worn across the shoulders, drinking animal fat or oil from a cow's horn. We could always tell when the men were getting ready to go on a raid because all the oil would be bought from the little mission kiosk. They drank the fat as they ran, not stopping even to rest for a day and a night or however long it took them to reach enemy territory, counting on the element of surprise as they would strike their enemy at first light, steal their cows and be gone before the enemy could muster forces to give chase.

On this morning they were not going to battle. There was no secrecy. The bells and chanting were meant to announce their coming. As they approached the mission, the people began to shout and cheer. In about two minutes the mission station had emptied. The women at the pump dropped their water jugs and ran for the road. The people waiting for treatment at the clinic dropped their clinic cards and ran, the mamas with their babies, the old men with their headaches, the sick and the well, the young and the old, the school children from the yard, the women who were waiting at the mill to grind their corn, the mama's cooking pots left unattended. In moments the little mission at Kiwawa looked like a ghost town.

I stood there alone wondering what was happening. And then I saw I was not alone. There was one young woman behind the school kitchen, squatting in the dirt in front of a dishpan, washing dishes. I walked over and saw that it was Elizabeth, one of our strong Christian women; in fact she had been our very first convert. I said, "Elizabeth, are you going?" "No, she said, I'm not going." It was then that I saw the tears streaming down her face.

I didn't understand what was going on but my curiosity drew me to the road and to the crowd gathered there. Then I saw what the people were cheering for: it was a group of young men, a war party of Pokot. They had just returned from tracking enemy spies. The Karamajong spies had been spotted sneaking through the mission, down a dry creek bed, just before dawn. A group of Pokot men had been quickly organized to give chase, They had caught up with the enemy and had killed them. Now returning victorious, they stopped at the end of the road to the mission and they dropped their spoils: the enemies' shoes, spears, a gun and some of the little carved wooden stools carried by all men in the bush to protect their bottoms from the thorns and to serve as a pillow for naps. The party was returning to a heroes' welcome. I looked at the young men; some were little more than boys who looked to be about 15. Some had made their first kill. The ones who had made a kill that day would be taken back to their villages and one side of their body, chest, back and arm to the elbow would be cut with arrows to form intricate patterns. Ashes would be rubbed into those cuts to create scars that, when healed, would resemble finely tooled leather. The scars would be worn proudly as a badge of honor for the rest of their lives. It would give them privileges in the villages, esteemed by the other warriors and admired by the young women. For Pokot young men it is like our athletes earning a letter in sports and wearing the jacket, showing the world what you have attained. Only for the Pokot, it was a very deadly sport.

Then I saw why Elizabeth was crying. Heading this party of warriors was her husband, one of the leading warriors in the area. His wife was one of the leading Christians, thus causing a great gulf between the two of them.

That night there would be singing in the village to honor these men, but Elizabeth would not be there. This was not the first time that Elizabeth's husband had killed. He was a seasoned warrior with many battles behind him. He had led many raids into Uganda to kill Karamajong people and to steal cows. Elizabeth had come to believe that the killing was wrong. Once, she had voiced her feelings when he was getting ready to go on a raid, and he beat her so badly that she lost the sight in one eye. Yet she never lost her stand for the Lord. Her new found faith had worked in her heart and had given her a peace that sustained her and a strong Christian testimony.

I walked back to the mission and saw this woman, so culturally different and yet so the same as me. I was always amazed that these women, underneath the goat skins, the tribal beads and the cow fat in their hair, were feminine, caring, hurting, romantic women. And the Lord works in their hearts just like He works in us: He changes lives, gives hope, gives joy, gives meaning to life. It doesn't matter if a person is in a goat skin or a Saks Fifth Avenue suit. The Lord's touch on a life is the same. If that isn't proof enough of God's existence, I don't know what is.

I went and put my arms around Elizabeth, and we hugged each other and shed a few tears together. I felt so bound to this woman. We all loved her. My first granddaughter is named after her. There was something else. We were soul sisters. I had cried my share of tears into the dishwater over the years, and for the same reasons. Oh, my husband didn't beat me or go steal cattle from the neighbors, but for 14 years we walked different roads and there was a great gap between us. I had cried with Elizabeth when her first-born son was four years old and her husband came and took him away to live with the warriors because he didn't want him to be raised as a Christian. I remembered my own sadness when my son thought it would be more fun to go fishing with his dad on Sundays than to go to church. When you've walked that road, your heart goes out to someone else on that difficult path of being submissive to both a husband and to the Lord when the paths are going in opposite directions. But God has His ways. When her husband forbade Elizabeth to come to women's fellowship at the mission, the women would go to her house afterwards and tell her everything that had been taught and pray with her. Her joy in the Lord and her quick engaging smile were always a precious testimony of her faith.

I would like to tell you that her life got better but it didn't. She had too hard a life and she died too young. One of her sons is strong in the Lord and now a Christian leader in the community. We know that there is a special place that Jesus prepared for her where there are no more tears and no more heartache. And someday I will be looking her up in Heaven to renew our sisterhood in glory.

> Eye has not seen, nor ear heard, nor have entered into the heart of man, the things which God has prepared for those who love Him. (I Corinthians 2:9)

Carolee and Elizabeth, best friends.

A typical Pokot compound with a hut for each wife, surrounded by a
thorn fence to keep livestock in at night and keep raiders and lions out.

Elizabeth with her newly framed house. The women do all the
work building, carrying water for mud, and the mudding.

The mud roof provides cool during the hot time of the year. In the
rainy season, it sometimes sprouts grass like a huge head of hair.

# Chapter 13

# The Walking Dead:
# The Famine of 1980

Then the King will say to those on His right hand,
'Come…inherit the kingdom prepared for you from the
foundation of the world: For I was hungry, and you gave
me food; I was thirsty, and you gave me drink.'
Matthew 25:34-35

It was like most mornings in the bush of Pokot land. I turned on the gas burner and put the coffee on. Glancing out the window, I was surprised to see a sad looking group of people sitting under a tree trying for some shade, but the tree had also suffered the effects of the drought and leaves were scarce. It was already hot and so dry. I looked out later as I sipped the first cup of coffee. The little group had grown to a small crowd so I walked out to see what the occasion was for such a gathering. As I approached, a woman rose and handed me a small child that looked and felt like a rag doll. The baby was already dead. My heart pounded as I realized what I was looking at. Everyone was so thin and many held children that looked like little skeletons: sad eyes, parched lips, skin in folds with little flesh beneath. The ever-present flies gathered around eyes and noses where there was no moisture left for the flies to steal. This group had walked out of Uganda looking for food on the Kenya side of the border. But there was no food here either. The rains had failed. The hard work of hand digging the soil and planting had brought nothing but disappointment and despair. People everywhere were hungry. By the end of the week our house was surrounded by hundreds of people in critical condition. We had no food to give them except the little on our shelves and it would not have begun to meet the need. In desperation we took pictures and headed to the city to look for help. At the World Vision office they took one look at the photos and immediately dispatched truck loads of food into the desert. The Christian women began cooking up the white ugali, a stiff porridge made from maize flour and soon a makeshift famine camp had sprung up in the middle of our mission compound, eventually feeding over a thousand people a day. We will never know how many lives were saved during the months of famine camp. The people we saw and the stories we heard were heart-breaking: children who had lost parents, mothers whose children had died on the way to the feeding camp, families torn apart by an enemy they could not fight. There was nothing in our experience that prepared us for the gut-wrenching tragedy that was famine.

*Anonymous poverty* was a phrase I learned from Pastor Moses who works among the poorest of the poor in Northern Uganda. Anonymous poverty: what an impact those words have. There are so many thousands out there living in day to day hunger and need; anonymous because the world seems unaware that they are even there. They have no voice. They have no way to be heard above the loud din of the world's televisions and commercials and violence and warfare in so many places. That silent cry of the dying child in that little skeleton body hardly makes a ripple on the world stage.

When sitting in a comfortable living room in the USA and the famine pleas come on the television, it is so easy just to change the channel. But when you wake up in your house in the desert of Africa and you look out your window and see people sitting under the trees in silent starvation, there is no way to turn it off. Like walking stick figures they come silently out of the bush. The silence of starving people is so eerie; no strength to cry they sit and wait, their last strength used up walking through the dust to a mission station where someone thought there might be hope. Our meager supplies would not even have made one meal for the multitude. The fact that no one rushed our house to take our food by force was amazing to me.

Over the next months we ran famine camps where our Christian women cooked up the white maize meal for thousands of people every day. The African staple *ugali* (maize meal mush) was the life saver for those people. We hauled maize meal into the outlying areas, sometimes by helicopter up into the remote mountains where there were no roads. Then when the life and death crisis subsided, we began food for work projects so people could do community projects in exchange for food to take home to their families. This continued for many months until the rains returned.

Then World Vision supplied seed so that the people could plant. Then pray. Pray that somehow the rains would come on time and would continue until the crops matured. That was the cycle of life for the Pokot people. Sometimes rain would come and the maize would spring up only to face weeks of no rain when the crops would wither and die. When more rain came, those who had seed left would frantically dig and plant again in hopes the rain would last long enough to bring a crop. Those of us who get our food from the grocery store don't have a clue what it is like to be totally dependent on undependable rain in this area bordering the Sahel region of Africa where famine is always lurking just around the corner with the next rainy season. Praise God for the organizations like International Disaster Emergency Service, World Vision and Food For The Hungry, who over the years responded and saved the lives of so many many people. As we would drive the one road that ran the length of Kara Pokot, we saw faces every day of people who would have been gone if not for help from the Western World. Later people would run out from villages to flag down our car to tell us that we saved their lives during the famine. School teachers, clinic workers, herders, policemen, flagged down our car to say, "Do you remember me? I came to Kiwawa when my family was starving." Only in eternity will we know the impact of that small act of providing, not a slice of bread, but a bowl of white maize meal mush that made the difference between life and death.

Lord, when did we see you hungry? (Matthew 25:37)

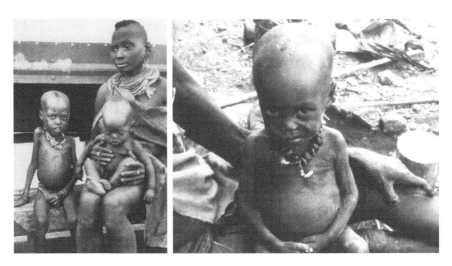

Famine is always hardest on the little ones and the very old.

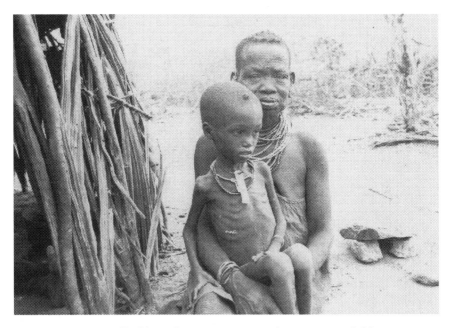

Mamas walked long distances carrying their starving children
to the feeding center at Kiwawa where help was available.

At the height of the famine, over 2,000 people were
being fed daily at the feeding camp.

Dick with some of the kids from the feeding camp.

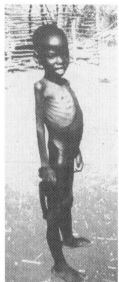

Naopei, so tiny that a jerry
can served as her bath tub.

Below: Naopei (on left) after the famine
in her new school uniform.

Jane Hamilton

*One Little Life*

Lou was about four when they came out of Uganda, part of a long line of walking dead. They were a little family whose members were one by one dropping along the way from hunger, from cholera, from dehydration, from exhaustion. Lou's mother and sister had both been lost on the way. About four years old and weighing only a skeletal 17 lbs with tiny match-stick arms and legs, Lou was very close to death himself. His father was a very old man with several wives. Lou's mother had been the youngest wife and her lifeless body was left along the trail.

It was a simple act: a desperate father handing a dying son off to a missionary at a feeding camp along the Kenya border. It had happened dozens of times during the famine. We had no idea that this one would be different; that no one would ever come to claim Lou, as usually happened with the famine orphans that were left with us. After a famine the family members would come seeking and claiming the children of their extended families, but no one ever came for Lou. Lou was destined to become part of our family and part of our lives. When Rosey Grier, one of the Los Angeles Rams "fearsome foursome," came to Kiwawa to do public relations for World Vision famine feeding, he connected with little Lou. As a result, Lou's picture with him appears on the back cover jacket of Rosey's autobiography. Lou's story was told far and wide and images of this little body appeared in World Vision magazines and on the IDES *Sonfish* banks raising funds for famine relief. He was the image of the success of the famine relief project and the many thousands of lives saved.

When it came time for us to go on furlough a few years later, we went through an adoption process in Kenya so that Lou could go to America with us. He was seven and very savvy. He had never talked about the famine. In fact for some months in the beginning, he never talked at all. We feared he had brain damage. He just sat quietly, mostly looking at the wall. Later he would tell me that he'd never been in a house before and didn't know what to say so he didn't say anything. (If that was really his memory or a cover-up, I will never know.) Once he did start talking, he made up for lost time. He was a very normal, mischievous happy little boy.

At age seven, Lou and I were packing his suitcase for the trip to America. I threw in a little plastic bag that held the leather neck charm he had been wearing the day his father gave him to us. Lou immediately took the bag out of the suitcase and threw it on the floor. I protested that it was all he had from his mother who had lovingly made it for him and that some day he would want it. His eyes filled with untypical tears as he said, "You didn't see me when I ate grass." We had no idea that he remembered the famine. No one ever spoke of it. Our memory of Lou had begun when he came to us. I didn't realize that his memory extended back to that awful trek across the desert, walking days without water or food, leaving his mother's cholera-racked body by the side of a dusty road, and in his memory "eating grass" to stay alive. So there we sat on the bed next to the suitcase, a white mother and a black son sharing tears over the painful memories that should not be in any child's memory bank. Then we put that chapter to rest and packed for safari.

That long walk was not the end of Lou's troubles. Years later, when we were forced to leave Kenya because of some political hassles, we were not allowed to take him with us. He spent some years living at the mission boarding school and then he went on to a boarding high school in the city. Later he went to Daystar University in the capital. We were able to support him from afar but could not be his close-up family. From twelve years old, he was pretty much on his own. One especially sad letter we received was when he was in high school and was making the long bus trip from the mission station in the bush to the boarding school in the city. He told us of someone having stolen his suitcase on the bus. Inside was his precious passport from when he had come to the US with us. It was his link to us and losing it took away his hope of rejoining us. It was the second time that mom and son had shared tears but this time we were on opposite sides of the world.

Despite all the difficulties and the years on his own, Lou grew into a fine young man. That tiny little skeleton that weighed only 17 pounds at four years old, grew into a 6' 4" giant who was captain of his college basketball team and went on to play on a Kenya national team. Eventually we were allowed back into Kenya and were able to once more be a family to Lou. He held a responsible government job in the capital city of Nairobi for many years and eventually returned to Kara Pokot to work for the mission, as his heart called him back to help his people.

As I think of Lou's life, I think once more of the unfairness of the "haves" and the "have-nots" of this world and how many children every day sit somewhere in the dirt and simply die because they are the "have-nots."

There are thousands of invisible children out there; children that we don't see "eating grass" or perhaps eating nothing at all. As God's people, His body, His hands and feet, it is our burden and our responsibility to share the bounty that we have with the have-nots of this world. As we thank God for our own abundance, let's give a thought to the "have-not" children of this world and the other little Lou's out there waiting for help.

> Then they also will answer Him, saying, 'When did we see you hungry . . . and did not minister to you?' Then He will answer them saying, . . . 'inasmuch as you did not do it to one of the least of these, you did not do it to me' (Matthew 25:44- 45)

Lou's father, after walking for many days looking for food for his family, handed Lou over to Dick with the request: "Make my son live." It was 1980 in the middle of a terrible famine when so many little ones did not have a chance to live.

Lou, at four years of age
weighed only 17 pounds and
was too weak to stand.

Lou, after famine feeding, a happy giggly kid

Lou, with Rosey Grier of the
Los Angeles Rams "Fearsome
Foursome" fame, during a visit
to Kiwawa feeding center.

Lou today, 6 foot four inches tall, size 13 shoe and was captain of his college basketball team at Daystar University.

"Big Lou", with Mom and Dad Hamilton, has grown
into a successful leader of the community.

*Aepoo*

The laughter came drifting through my kitchen window as I was doing the morning dishes. I looked out the window to see Aepoo and Lou, rolling down the hill behind our little mud house and crawling back up to roll down again. Two little five-year olds, one crippled by polio and one orphaned by famine, having the time of their lives. I leaned out to see what could possibly be so funny. To my amazement they were hurling insults at each others fathers. These were fathers that neither of them could remember ever having in their lives, but for some reason they were getting great sport calling each others' father a baboon and a hyena, and a few other choice words I could not translate. The wild giggling of these two little imps was sweet music to my ears.

I thought how like any little boy anywhere in the world finding macho things to do, here they were making teasing insults about each others fathers. These two little tykes had been given a very rough deal in life but they were so full of the life they had and the simple joy of being alive. Aepoo's polio had left him with shriveled up little legs, one leg could only dangle between the crutches, but what a little man he was. He was the tough one of the two. He could always make Lou cry by telling stories about hyenas coming in at night to drag kids into the bush. The two were inseparable and remained friends throughout their lives, even after Lou grew to six foot four and Aepoo never topped five feet. Lou always looked out for his little buddy.

The first time we saw Aepoo he was about three years old; his mother struggled to carry him juggling a newborn cradled in her arms. She had carried Aepoo for several years but now it was no longer possible to carry him with a new baby to care for. She flagged our car down and we thought she wanted to ask us for a ride, but that was not her mission. She simply handed this little crippled boy through the window of our car and hurried off. We had heard stories of polio victims just being left in the bush to whatever fate would take them first: lions, hyenas or starvation. That is the hard reality for nomadic people in the bush where there is no way to care for a crippled child. And so our little house at the mission had become a place where polio kids could find refuge. Sometimes their little legs needed surgery to straighten the twisted limbs, which meant being taken to a hospital in the city. Sometimes they just needed tiny little crutches to be able to get around. Mostly they needed love and food and a place to belong.

I doubt that Aepoo had ever been in a vehicle before that day his mom handed him off to us. He fought and hollered the whole trip, protesting his abduction, as we made our way up the escarpment to the base house in Kitale. When we arrived, I set him down in the driveway while I unloaded the car. Then two huge Rhodesian Ridgeback hounds came racing around the corner of the house. Aepoo quickly scooped up as many rocks as he could reach and began pelting the dogs. That was Aepoo. He was born with a warrior's heart and it served him well throughout his life.

He played soccer with the other school kids, crutches flying, never fearing the inevitable falls, only concerned with being competitive with the kids whose legs worked. We never heard Aepoo complain or make excuses. He was one tough little guy.

As an adult we started him in a little kiosk (shop) for the village, where he could earn a living. He always had a ready smile and a joke, living life to the full as best he could. Aepoo married and became the father of two daughters, beautiful little girls that he adored. Whenever a vehicle was leaving Kiwawa to go anywhere in the bush, you would find Aepoo hitching a ride to get in on the action. Everyone loved Aepoo for the strong spirit inside of him that overcame his physical limitations. As he got older, he was often in and out of the hospital, his body weakening every year. He fought off bouts of the ever-present malaria and eventually he succumbed to pneumonia. We lost a good friend and a bright spot in our lives. We will look for him in Heaven . . . without the crutches.

Aepoo on the parallel bars, struggling to walk.

Aepoo, legs crippled by polio but the grit of a
warrior, a ready smile and an open heart

Kemoi, Lou and Aepoo in 1981

Lou, Aepoo and Kemoi stayed buddies over the years

Into Africa

*Special Visitors:*

Our association with *World Vision* brought many fascinating people into our lives. Several times a year the organization would bring groups out to see the work, first of famine feeding and then the child sponsorship program. The most exciting to us was Rosey Grier of the "fearsome foursome" Los Angeles Rams fame. Being avid football fans, it was a big deal for us to have one of the greats visit our little mission in the bush of Africa. He was the nicest man, humble and unassuming. The way he interacted with the children was awesome. He brought a guitar and sang songs for the kids. A lot of events, in a place with no calendars, were remembered as: "before Rosey" or "after Rosey." Him being such a giant of a man and being the same color as the kids, made him an instant hit. He spent time just sitting with the children and playing guitar; when he left he gave his guitar to one of the school boys.

Rosey wasn't a fan of flying but he got into a little bush plane and landed at a small airstrip about 40 miles north of Kiwawa. Dick picked him up there to drive him to the station. Dick was legendary (or notorious?) for the way he drove the bush roads, flying over the ruts and bumps, his theory being that you could skim over the washboard if you drove fast enough. On the way, Rosey gave him some much-needed advice. With his big arm span, Rosey was able to sit with one arm on the passenger-side window and reach across with his other arm to pat Dick on the shoulder facing the driver side window and, in his big deep voice, say: "*slow down, Parnelli.*" It was a quote we all used in later years to try to get Hamilton to slow down.

We had Rosey autograph the headboard of the bed: "Rosey slept here." Unfortunately we did not get back to the USA with that piece of memorabilia, but we have great memories of a special blessing, being with someone of his stature, both size and heart.

Rosey with the Hamiltons in front of the black and white tree in
the river bed near Kiwawa. The unusual black and white tree was
symbolic to the people of our partnership with them in ministry.

Rosey, sharing a few quiet moments with Lou.

Big Rosey with the school children at Kiwawa.

Jane Hamilton

Rosey Grier's visit to the children of Kiwawa was a major event in their lives. (And also for Carolee who was a great football fan.)

Other visitor groups included the wife of one of our astronauts, an executive of Cargill (one of the largest privately owned corporations in the world), and Jim Peterson, an insurance executive from Minnesota, who was so impressed with our program of charging ten percent of the maize ground in the corn mill to feed school children, that he became a sponsor.

One of the biggest events was when Carol Lawrence, Hollywood star singer and dancer, came to do a documentary of the famine feeding program. During the time the film crew was there, a cattle raid took place just down the road and the crew rushed off to film the carnage left behind. Carol was nonplussed through all of the real life drama, a real trooper. The film *Crisis in the Horn of Africa* raised millions of dollars in the US. Out of that money came the big Rift Valley Water Project which opened a whole new chapter in our lives. That story is told elsewhere in this book.

Carol's assistant followed her around trying to keep her shaded under an umbrella from the hot African sun, but her focus was on the children. She held starving babies with diarrhea, she dished up food for kids at the famine feeding station, she held the hand of a mother whose baby was near death from dehydration and told the mom, "all mothers feel the same things." At one point, she entered into a dance with Chepateltel, not knowing that she was the local crazy lady. In the midst of the dance, Chepateltel went into a trance and fell backward. Carol was holding one of the missionary children, and swung an arm to protect the child. In the photo it looks like she had just slapped the person falling backward. Seeing is not always believing. It is one of our favorite pictures.

Carol Lawrence's encounter with Chepateltel.

### Welcome to the end of the earth

Gary Wiessner, a former oil company executive was the *World Vision* executive who brought the first visitor group from Minnesota out to Kiwawa, and he became a life-long friend. His brother-in-law was news anchor at one of the big Chicago TV stations and they came to do a documentary on the 1980 famine. Chuck Henry gave us one of the most memorable quotes that stuck with us at Kiwawa. When he got off the helicopter he said: "This may not be the end of the earth but I'm sure you can see it from here." His newscasts brought the national spotlight to our little corner of the world and the suffering of the Pokot people during that desperate famine time. Many thousands of lives were saved due to the attention of *World Vision, International Disaster Emergency Service (IDES), Food for the Hungry* and the donors in USA who responded to the needs of the people. Walking around Pokot today you can see so many people who would not be alive if not for this compassionate outreach. The heart of the American people to help the suffering of the world is amazing.

When we went to Pokot land we thought we were going into a forgotten place and would be lost in the wilderness of need and anonymous suffering of the people. World Vision's response to those needs brought us into contact with some of the world's most interesting people. We treasure those years and memories.

Gary Wiessner, inspecting the output flow from a newly drilled well, sponsored by World Vision International.

# Chapter 14

# A Cattle Raid at Losam

You shall not be afraid of the terror by night, nor of the
arrow that flies by day.
Psalms 91:5

*December 1980*

We were just sitting down for breakfast with a World Vision film crew when news came down the road of a cattle raid in progress at the neighboring village of Losam. The storm clouds of raiding and warfare had been gathering for some time but this was to be a memorable day.

The Mission station at Kiwawa was located on the Uganda border and that had created many insecure situations with Karamojong cattle raiders crossing the border to steal Pokot cattle. The raiding became especially deadly in the 1980s when Uganda dictator Idi Amin Dada, known as the butcher of Uganda, after causing about 300,000 deaths in his 8 year reign, got on a helicopter and fled Uganda. The world breathed a sigh of relief, but for us living four miles from the Uganda border, it was just the beginning of a short reign of terror in our little corner of Kenya. Just across the border in Moroto, Amin had an outpost armory full of automatic weapons. The Karamojong warriors, traditional enemies of the Pokot, who had been carrying on warfare for generations with spears and bows and arrows, broke into Amin's abandoned armory and were suddenly in possession of AK-47s, and even rocket launchers. The mode of cattle raiding and tribal fighting took an ugly turn as the balance of power tilted in favor of the Karamojong. The enemy of the Pokot were now heavily armed, while the Pokot had only their traditional spears and bow and arrows. To make matters worse some of Idi Amin's henchmen joined up with the Ugandan cattle raiders. It was a time of great insecurity for the region. Unfortunately, it was also a time of famine. Some organizations doing famine relief were forced to pack up and go. Several nuns were killed at a mission on the Uganda side of the border and the newly armed Karamajong were running amok with their powerful weapons. As the fighting became more brutal, the insecurity along the border became untenable.

We prayed and pondered about what to do. Shutting down the famine feeding would mean many people would simply starve. We were feeding several thousand people daily and many of those were children and elderly people who would have suffered terribly without the help. We struggled with the safety issue and prayed earnestly for God's direction. Staying there put us and our entire staff at risk, as well as the school children in the dormitories.

In times of stress, I always turned to my personal "therapist": the book of Psalms. So, as I struggled with the decision, my Bible fell open one morning to Psalm 22. Verses 27 - 31 read: "All the ends of the earth will remember and turn to the Lord. And all the families of the nations will worship before Thee. For the kingdom is the Lord's. . . . all the prosperous of the earth will eat and worship . . .Posterity will serve Him; it will be told of the Lord to the coming generation. They will come and will declare His righteousness to a people yet unborn." Several phrases jumped off the page at me. "All the ends of the earth." (Remembering Chuck Henry's comment when he got off the helicopter and said, "This may not be the end of the earth but I'm sure you can see it from here.") That phrase, "the end of the earth" really fit the remoteness of our area. The other phrase that jumped out at me was "the prosperous of the earth will eat and worship." Then there was the last part about "declaring His righteousness to a people yet unborn." Reading this verse was a personal reassurance to me that we were doing the right thing by staying, for the future generations of Pokot yet to be born. For Dick there was never any thought of leaving. If I had gone to safer territory, I'm sure he would have stayed to keep the famine camp going. He was totally committed and always ready for whatever God destined for us. His standard comment to us was "My bags are packed." And he wasn't talking about leaving; he was talking about being ready for God to take him home.

So we planted our feet for the long haul: gun shots heard in the night, casualties coming into the clinic, constant rumors circulated of impending raids and many sleepless nights. For whatever reason, Kiwawa Mission was never attacked. Daily famine feeding continued. Eventually the Pokot, who were superior warriors, captured guns from the Karamojong and bought guns from Ethiopia. The balance of power gradually equalized, but the culture and the lifestyle of the Pokot forever changed after the transition to guns.

## World Vision Visitors Caught in the Raid

As news came of the Karamajong cattle raid in progress at Losam, we learned that several thousand raiders had crossed the border to steal cows and were killing people at the village. Our staff grabbed medical boxes and headed toward the village with the World Vision people and the film crew in tow. They got to the village as the raiders were retreating and were able to treat some of the wounded. In the midst of drought the people were devastated to have lost their only source of life, their herds of cattle that had been taken. During the dry time the Pokot survive by bleeding the cattle and mixing the blood with milk for a protein drink that literally keeps them alive. (This drink was dubbed by Dick a *Pokot strawberry milkshake*.) Stan Mooneyham, World Vision President, quickly promised to provide food for the families until the rains returned. But the loss of their cattle was a major crisis for the people of Losam.

Meanwhile I was "safe" back at Kiwawa, far from the raiding, but shortly we heard shots behind the mission and realized some of the retreating raiders were coming right towards us. The women and school kids grabbed me (the only white person left at the mission) and pulled me up a hill behind the station. The women wrapped my head with a dark scarf so my blonde hair would not draw raiders' attention. They showed me not to run in the dry creek bed where raiders might be running but to crawl through the thorn brush hidden from sight. We hid on the top of the hill until near dark when the crew returned from Losam and the helicopter landed with actress Carol Lawrence and others to film the documentary.

The sadness of that day was the death of one of our young men. I had been talking with him when the shots rang out but he refused to run with us to the hills. He had been through his manhood rites and he could not run away. He had to go toward the fighting, even though he was unarmed. The warrior code of protecting the tribe at all costs was honored and it took his life that day when he was shot by the raiders. He was one of the sons of our head man, Loitaluk. He had been to school, spoke good English and had been hired at the clinic as a translator. Pastor John had given him a Pokot New Testament and he was in the new converts' class eagerly learning scripture verses. Because of his bright mind and eager spirit John had great hopes for him as a Christian leader. His death was a terrible loss to the community, but here was the victory: our medical work and famine feeding only keep bodies going a little longer on this old earth; but salvation is for eternity. We called this young man "The Six Million Dollar Man" because he wore a bright red T-shirt with that inscription. We know that in eternity he will be one of many Pokot there with the Lord because of the outreach of the little mission at Kiwawa.

The film of the famine feeding and the Losam raid aired in the U.S. as *The Crisis in the Horn of Africa*. It starred singer/actress Carol Lawrence. The film raised millions of dollars. Stan Mooneyham, the President of *World Vision International*, called and asked what do the Pokot people need? Dick's reply was WATER. Out of that money came funding for the Rift Valley Water Project which opened a whole new chapter in our lives. Over 150 water wells were drilled. But a tragic side of that story is told in another chapter.

Rosey Grier had shared a humorous story of how, as a defensive lineman, he picked up a fumble and found out that a loose football draws a mean ugly crowd. We found out that big funding and expensive drilling equipment does draw a mean crowd and in the years that followed the blessing that God provided for the Pokot people brought with it some heartbreaking tragedy for our mission family.

> Be strong and courageous. Do not be afraid or tremble. The Lord your God is the one who goes with you. He will not fail you or forsake you. (Duet 31:6)

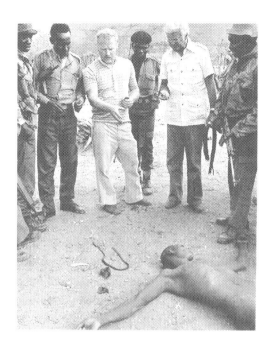

Dick and Stan Mooneyham, President of World Vision, viewing the body of one of the Karamajong raiders that was killed by the Kenya army.

The introduction of guns into the culture changed tribal warfare into a more deadly conflict for the tribes who had traditionally done battle with spears and bows and arrows.

# Chapter 15

# Death in Kenya – A Martyr's Story

Who shall separate us from the love of Christ? Shall
tribulation, or distress, or persecution, or famine, or
nakedness, or peril, or sword? As it is written, For your
sake we are killed all day long; we are accounted as sheep
for the slaughter. Yet in all these things we are more
than conquerors through Him who loved us. For I am
persuaded that neither death, nor life, nor angels, nor
principalities, nor things present, nor things to come,
nor powers, nor height, nor depth, nor any other created
thing, shall be able to separate us from the love of God,
which is in Christ Jesus our Lord.

Romans 8:35-39

*September 1986*

With the new water project funded by World Vision, more help was needed and volunteers stepped forward. One of them was our long time friend, Lyle Hutson, a big man with a vise-like hand shake and a hearty laugh that just made you feel good. Lyle had been our neighbor in Oregon, an elder in our church and a precious friend. He had been involved with the mission from the beginning. Ten years earlier his big truck rolled up to our door to load household goods headed for Seattle when Dick enrolled in Bible College. Lyle and Leta Mae served as forwarding agents the early years of the mission. He had always been a driving force for the outreach to Kenya and even though he had a heart condition, he dreamed of someday being on the mission field himself. He had retired from his business after owning an aggregate business, and had been a driller and powder monkey who could charge up a hill with a 90-lb bag under each arm. Lyle never met a stranger and reached out to everyone he met. He jumped right in and took charge of the packing of the containers for the drilling project, excited to see his life-long dream of mission work fulfilled.

In Kenya, Lyle was gloriously happy as he worked making equipment, modifying hand pumps, and getting ready for the drilling project. His time spent with the Christians in Pokot was a precious time. He fixed crutches and wheelchairs, taught leadership training classes and loved the people as only Lyle could love – with bear hugs and hearty handshakes. He gave freely to everyone who needed it. When the new drilling equipment arrived on the docks of Mombasa, we were all excited to receive the machines and the goods of the new families coming to work on the water project. But Satan never sleeps and he never misses an opportunity to spoil God's work.

For six months a special branch of the Central Intelligence Department and the Port Police had been searching incoming freight at Mombasa Port looking for guns which the Kenya government feared were being smuggled into the country to attempt to overthrow President Moi's government. Unfortunately when our containers were opened by Kenya customs in Mombasa, they found items that set off a nation-wide panic. Air pistols and air rifles which families had put in for snake and rodent control were mistaken for automatic weapons. The school uniforms were classified as military uniforms. The fly paper rolls were listed as shot gun shells. The digital bath scale was taken as evidence of something but they weren't sure what. Even a child's toy gun that shot ping pong balls was confiscated. It would have been comical if it had not ended so tragically.

The national newspaper headlines announced that a shipment of arms had been intercepted and a plot to overthrow the government had been stopped. On September 19th, while Dick was still in Mombasa trying to clear the freight, Lyle and our teenage son Rick were picked up in Kitale and held overnight in the jail. They had arrested Rick by mistake because he is named after his dad so his passport read Richard Hamilton Jr. They were looking for Richard Hamilton Sr., but we could not convince them they had the wrong guy. The next day they were transported to Nairobi and placed in a cell in abominable conditions. Urine ran across the floor from an overflowing toilet in the communal bathrooms next to their cell. No bed, no chairs, just a cold wet cement floor. The three days they were held were full of hardship, incredible tension and anxiety. The weekend was a nightmare with Lyle's wife, Leta Mae, and I trying to get someone at the Embassy to get help for Lyle. We knew he was in medical trouble but no one took us seriously. We tried to take a foam mattress to the jail so he could lay down but the Matron told us, "This is a jail not a hotel." She told us it would be discrimination to let a white prisoner have a mattress when the others didn't. We begged for his health. She said that even food was a privilege and if we continued to bother her she would take away their shoes. We left in tears to the laughter of the guards. It was the only time I saw Leta Mae shed any tears. She was a strong lady. Later a friend did help us get a mattress in after the guards had changed for the night. He picked it up early in the morning so Lyle had one night of rest out of the three days in the jail cell.

Sunday afternoon Lyle preached for two hours to the other prisoners. He ministered to them. He took down names of prisoners in the jail who wanted their families contacted. He even gave away his Bible. We learned later that Lyle had given away the food we had taken him because he couldn't eat with all those hungry eyes watching him. There were female prisoners and young children in the jail, and Lyle just could not eat his food in front of the hungry children. He said later that he thought he knew how Jesus had survived without food in the wilderness because Lyle said he felt that the Holy Spirit was feeding him and he never felt hungry. But though Lyle's spirit was strong, his heart condition could not handle the stress of those days and nights of harsh confinement, and the shock of having the people he had gone to help accuse him of trying to overthrow the government. It took a tremendous toll on Lyle's already weakened heart.

Finally, on Monday morning they were released and told to report the next morning to the Central Intelligence Department. By that time the CID realized that a mistake had been made. That night at the hotel we had a celebration dinner with Lyle and some World Vision visitors who were there touring Kenya. Lyle was in great spirits. He said he felt he could relate to Paul and the experiences he had had in jail. He joked about having a "captive audience" to preach to.

Tuesday morning Dick, Lyle and Rick reported to the CID Headquarters. We thought it was routine and they would be released. We had already received a verbal apology though nothing was ever put in writing to correct the terrible mistake they had made. Sitting in the CID Headquarters, Lyle looked at the morning newspaper where the press had picked up the story. The headlines told of President Moi accusing the missionaries of undermining security. Lyle read the headlines and slumped over in Dick's arms. Rick ran the three blocks to the hotel to get Leta Mae who placed nitroglycerin tablets under his tongue, but Lyle was gone.

The coroners report said that Lyle's heart was bad and that he could have gone at any time. The autopsy showed that his heart was large and bore many scars from previous damage. That was true in another sense, for all who knew Lyle knew him to be a big-hearted man who had borne the scars that life handed him with dignity and faith. Lyle died as he lived, faithfully serving his Lord in a positive, up-beat frame of mind. Against the odds and in the worst of times, Lyle could always see some humor and something to praise God for in every situation. Lyle went to be with the Lord he loved and served, even unto death. He died a martyr. He died a hero. Through it all Lyle never lost his witness.

The Kenya news stories were picked up by the Associated Press and many things were printed that were simply not true. Nothing found in the freight was illegal. Air guns could be purchased in downtown Nairobi over the counter without a permit. The machine guns and army uniforms reported in the paper were harmless air guns that shot be bees and pellets. The uniforms were children's school uniforms sown by church women in the USA. The maps marked potential drilling sites, and the camping equipment (army surplus type) was for use on the drilling sites. Other items confiscated were things they could not identify like a digital bath scale, battery tester, smoke alarms, a thermal coffee cup, and rolls of fly paper.

We never received any official clearance or apology from the Kenya government. We were just told not to talk to the press and to go back to work. It took many months and much patience for the shipment to finally be released to us and we were able to go forward with the drilling. We reminded ourselves that our war was with Satan and not the Kenya government or officials.

After the equipment was released we were able to drill over 150 wells during the span of the Rift Valley Water Project. We think of those wells as memorials to Lyle, providing life-giving water to the people he went to serve.

In the dark hours after Lyle's death so many "why" questions could not be answered. It all seemed so senseless. In our pain for Leta Mae and their four children, everyone shared their grief in some way. During that time a friend came to me and shared this thought. The scripture often talks of Jesus being seated at the right hand of God. But as Stephen was being stoned to death the Bible says he looked into Heaven and he saw Jesus STANDING at the right hand of God. As Stephen was being martyred Jesus was fully engaged and was standing . . . watching and waiting to welcome Stephen into Heaven's embrace. The friend suggested that we could visualize Lyle being welcomed into Heaven. There was comfort in that thought for me. Family members shared that they knew Lyle died doing what he had always dreamed of doing. And when we get to Heaven we will be able to see it from God's point of view, and then perhaps there won't be any pain associated with the memories.

In the aftermath of it all we clung to the scripture: "We press on . . . toward the high calling of the Gospel of Christ." And so we pressed on . . . drilled wells . . . established schools and clinics . . . ministered and taught.

In a memorial service held in Nairobi for Lyle, a Presbyterian Bishop said, "Lyle's death did more for the church in Kenya than if he had drilled a thousand wells." He referred to Lyle as, "this brother who gave his life for our people." We believe that Lyle's life was not given in vain and that only in eternity will we know the full reach of his sacrifice.

Lyle Malven Hutson, May 28, 1923 – September 24, 1986

These things I have spoken to you, that in Me you may have peace. In the world you will have tribulation, but be of good cheer, I have overcome the world. (John 16:33)

Lyle and Leta Mae Hutson in Kenya

Well done, good and faithful servant. (Matthew 25:23)

# Chapter 16

## Encamped About

The angel of the Lord encamps all around those who fear
Him, and delivers them
Psalms 34:7

*A Page from the Diary - February 28, 1988*

"Encamped about" . . . words that appear in the Old Testament. Not much
meaning attached to them in Twentieth century America, but tonight, here
in the bush of Africa, they have powerful meaning.

On any ordinary evening, I sit on my porch and look out at the little fires
on the hillsides that represent the villages scattered on the hills and valleys
that surround Kiwawa Mission. "Encamped about." Those fires represent
security. But tonight there are no fires on the hills, no sound of cattle or
pumping wells, no sound of children in the dormitories. The mission station
is deserted except for a few staff. Inside my house are 12 children, most of
them crippled by polio, the only children left here. The other 400 are hiding
out in the bush.

The men assure me that it is only a "panic" and that there is no real
danger. So we stay. And we wait. We try to demonstrate our faith in God
by not panicking. A few moments ago the boys heard the warriors signal
across the far hill saying "be ready." A few of our Pokot warriors are still
out there. Too few. But enough to sound the alarm and give us time to run.
Unfortunately, the little polio kids cannot run. So we wait. I am the only
white person here on the station. And there are only three women: myself,
nurse Jenifer from the clinic and Jane, an African visitor from upcountry
who is not used to the cattle raids and insecurity of the bush. Both women
have gone to sleep. The two school boys who are my night watchmen have
stayed, but when the other boys left the dormitories to go to the hills, I

could see by the looks on their faces they would have liked to have joined that party. But they will stay with me. They have only bows and arrows for weapons, but they will stay. The night is so strangely quiet. Only the sound of the wind. A moon bright enough to see very clearly. A "raiders' moon," they call it here.

Someone just came to tell me that no Karamajong warriors have been sighted. "It is only a panic." "Don't worry." The "panic" started a few weeks ago when some Karamajong raided some cows near here. Some of our Christians lost their cattle in that raid. Then a few days ago another raid and more cows were taken near the mission. The men began to move all the herds away from the border and into the hills. With the cattle went the warriors who guard them. Then the families moved out of the villages. Now there is no one left between Kiwawa and the border. This afternoon the wives of our staff took their children and headed for safer ground. The girls' dormitory followed suit; then the three dormitories of younger boys. I looked in one dorm where a lantern was still burning, study books left open, clothes where they had dropped, but no kids. It looked like the rapture had just taken place. The bigger boys who were going to stay finally left when they heard the "be ready" warning signal. Perhaps they went to "be ready" and join the fight.

My little charges have finally settled down to sleep after cups of tea and reassurances. They get so afraid when everyone runs and they are left behind. What a tough life these kids have. Jesus' little sheep. It will be a long night. I reassure myself that God has always protected us. In ten years, the station has never been attacked; and on this beautiful moonlit night, I can't think of anywhere else in the world I'd rather be than right here. And maybe we are "encamped about" after all. By unseen protectors. "God is our shield" the Psalms says. About dawn we hear the bird call signal from the warriors in the river bed that all is clear. And the sun comes up on the stillness of another day in this little corner of God's world.

**Post note:** How the sweet Holy Spirit brings to mind the scriptures that nurture and comfort us in times of trial and testing. There in the darkness and insecurity of that night, God wrapped me in a blanket of peace and security. Once more that wonderful "peace that passes understanding," God's special gift to His own, came to rest on my heart.

And the Peace of God, which surpasses all understanding, will guard your hearts and minds through Christ Jesus. (Philippians 4:7)

Yea, though I walk through the valley of the shadow of death, I fear no evil; for You are with me; Your rod and Your staff, they comfort me. (Psalms 23:4)

E.T., Lou and Aepoo, some of Kiwawa's precious "little sheep" who could
not run when there were warnings of raiders. Warm cups of tea and
calm assurances provided comfort as we waited out the long nights.

Tiny crutches and braces
for little Polio victims.

My friend Sharon Christian said that I should change my name to "Indiana Jane." It had been that kind of a year.

Shortly after the all-night raid vigil, I was on my way out of Kiwawa when we drove into the middle of a raid in progress. We didn't know it was happening as we had stopped for a bush break at the dry river bed. We were out of the car when we saw some warriors running towards us. Fortunately they were Pokot and not the enemy. A boy about 14 years old had been shot in the fighting. The bullet had entered the right side of his back, gone out the left side and shattered his elbow. They loaded him, bleeding badly, into the back of my car. It took three long hours to reach the hospital. If I drove fast, every bump in the road caused him to writhe in pain and going slowly I feared he would bleed to death. Fortunately the bullet had just passed through his flesh and had not hit his spine or vital organs. The worst injury was the elbow that had permanent damage, but a week later he was walking around the hospital ward on the way to recovery.

After the cattle raid scares and the ambulance run, I was on my way back to Kiwawa when I had the misfortune to hit a washed out gully in the road that sent my car careening to the edge, balancing over a deep ravine. Alone in the desert with a broken car and a banged-up leg, the only help were my school boy passengers who were trying to stop the bleeding from my nose and knee. I began to do some real soul searching. Before I had time to go into panic mode, a truck came by with a couple of Somali traders who gave me a ride up the escarpment to get help. That was one of those *divine coincidences*, because it might have been days before anyone passed that way. They dropped me at the first little clinic at the top of the escarpment where two Kenyan male *dressers* (nurses) were determined to sew me up. I was able to get a message sent to Dick to come rescue me, while I tried to hold these guys at bay from stitching me up in very unsanitary conditions. Soiled dressings and used needles littered the floor and it didn't seem like the place I wanted to be stitched. I kept telling them I had to wait for my husband. When Dick and my brother Jim finally arrived, they scooped me up and ran for the car, with the nurses running up the path after us shouting that they had not treated me yet and I needed to be stitched. I'm sure it must have looked like something out of a slap-stick comedy, with us running for the road with two white-coated fellows in hot pursuit. Nine hours after the guys rescued me and towed the car, I found myself laying in the emergency room of a little private hospital in Kitale getting 13 stitches and waiting for the x-ray technician to be located at a nearby bar, finally to learn that my leg was broken.

There were times I wished for a rest from the hectic pace but six weeks immobilized was a little too much rest. I was more than ready to get back to work so I hitched a ride with Leroy on the truck taking supplies to Kiwawa. After my two previous *exciting* trips, I thought this one would be routine. On the return trip we crossed the river at flood stage and hit some quicksand. The truck went down, the water came up and Leroy went swimming. He was trying desperately to carry the children riding in the bed of the truck to safety and to attach a chain on the front bumper which was quickly sinking into the sand. I was on the high side of the cab and the water was at my waist and rising. Holding camera bag, briefcase and purse above my head, I considered my prospects. I could see men standing knee deep off to the side but the current was swift and I didn't know if I could keep my footing or be washed down stream. Before I had to make that hard decision, a group of the Pokot men formed a human chain and came to my rescue, pulling me through the window and carrying both me and my possessions to safety.

As the truck was sinking and shifting toward its side, the driver of the government road grader that was standing by to pull us out decided he needed to turn around. It seemed for sure that the truck would be lost to the river. Just at the last minute the chain was secured and the grader began to pull. Another of those divine coincidences, that there happened to be a road grader there at that time to pull the truck to safety. The big Bedford Lorry (truck), the lifeline of Kiwawa Mission, was spared to continue its job of providing supplies for the Lord's work in Pokot. Praise God for watching out for us. The next day a trader's truck, loaded with bags of cement, was washed on its side and swept downriver.

The old Bedford mission truck, moments before it was pulled to
safety. The Kanyangerang River is dry most of the year but during
the rainy season many days and nights were spent on the river
bank waiting for the water to go down for safe crossing.

# Chapter 17

## Warriors' Tales

…having the everlasting gospel to preach to those who
dwell on the earth – to every nation, tribe, tongue and
people.
Revelation 14:6b

The Pokot people of western Kenya are a fascinating tribe. The reason we
see them in history books as the *Suk* is because that is the name they gave
the British in colonial times. *Suk* means a stick or an old dead log, a tree
that is downed and rotting, of no use. They just wanted the British-ruled
government of Kenya to go away and leave them alone. Their real name
is *Pokot*, which means hospitality. Now you may think that hospitality is a
strange name for a warrior tribe. In truth they are a warm, hospitable people.
They will kill their last chicken to cook a meal for a visitor. They will use
their last tea to fix a drink for a traveler. We have been the humble recipients
of both of those sacrifices on the part of the poorest of the poor.

The Pokot warriors are strong and swift. Their survival depends on
them being vigilant, alert and ready for action at all times. They can run for
hours when going to a raid or when fleeing from enemy raiders. You never
saw a warrior without his traditional two spears. . .sharpened, honed and
ready for battle, and in later years, the AK 47 slung over one shoulder.

With no television or radio, the pastime at night for the young men was
to tell the tales of warriors and battles: the intrigue of the spying and cattle
raiding, and the bravery of the warriors. Of course in every culture and every
people there are exceptions. There was one young man, friendly and likable,
but not quite in the mold of the ready warrior. Around the fires at night as
the stories would be told of the brave feats of battle, if laughter broke out
you knew that a story was being told of this kid. He was brave enough, just
not always prepared.

One day when the Karamajong raiders came, he went forth with his bow and arrows. When he spotted an enemy in front of him, he quickly let fly with an arrow in the enemy's direction, but the feathers on his arrow had not been tended in a long time and his arrow arched up, fluttered and fell pitifully short and off course. All he managed to do was draw the attention of the enemy warrior, at which point he cried, "uncle, uncle" for his relative who was behind him armed with a gun. His uncle stepped out from behind a nearby tree and came to his rescue. With every telling of this story, hand gestures would trace the flight of the miserable unkempt arrow and howls of laughter would ring out. Later this young man acquired an old gun. When the soldiers came making a sweep of Pokot to seize the guns (it is illegal for a private citizen in Kenya to own a gun), we found his gun hidden in our outdoor shower. Fortunately, the soldiers did not search our house.

One of our older men, who had built his huts near the mission, had been a warrior. After becoming a Christian he gave up his warrior ways. While the truck load of army guys searched the compound, this stately old man stood leaning on the truck chatting with the driver. He was probably the only one who really had guns and they were well hidden where the soldiers would not discover them. We were amused at his cool, just standing talking to the driver when his own weapons were nearby.

Some very sad incidents happened on those sweeps when the army came looking for the Pokot guns. There were beatings and violence by the army but the Pokot never turned in their guns during those raids. Once we heard the men laughing saying they had just told the soldiers, "Beat us some more, we like it." They were a tough lot.

The army's only effective anti-gun campaign was when they rounded up the cows and took them into custody, telling the warriors they would only get their cows back when they turned in their guns. Sadly the army did not water or care for the livestock and some died in the pens where they were being held. Many guns were turned in during that army operation because the men could not tolerate seeing their cows die. To save their suffering cattle, the men were forced to turn in their guns. Despite all the government efforts to disarm the Pokot, there remained lots of guns and when the Karamajong raiders from Uganda came for cattle we were always grateful that the Pokot did have their guns. It gave us the safety we needed along the border to stay and work in that tribal war zone.

Today the governments of Kenya and Uganda are working together to stop the cattle raiding and killing. There are far fewer raids and deaths than in the old days. All of this changes the culture drastically. In the history of the Pokot, the young men would have to raid for cattle to pay the bride price for their wives. No cows, no wives. When cows were exchanged for wives, the family and community recognized and enforced the marriage bond. If the wife went back to mama, the cattle bride price paid for her would have to be returned. Of course, the father of the family would never agree to return the cows. The wife would always be returned to the husband. It was a stable, binding system though not advantageous for the women who were in effect *sold* to their husbands. It did represent an obligatory agreement that was foundational to the society. Today without those traditional trappings, the morals are looser and the young people are not always held to the old traditional standards. Hopefully the Christian standards of one wife and married for life will replace the old ways. It is certainly better for the women of the society to be free to marry for love, but when the physical relationship comes before the marriage it has same effects of breaking down morals and family systems that we find in western culture.

Living in Pokot land in the early days was a bit like the old west in America. There were always rumors of spies being sighted and footprint tracks where Karamajong spies had been near the villages looking for cows. Many stories were told of the shoot-outs that took place. Then, of course, we would see the results come into the clinic. Guys with spears through their bodies and then later the gun shot wounds. Trying to get a guy with a spear still sticking through his body into the helicopter to airlift him out was a real challenge. The stories they told of the heroes of battle always sounded glamorous and exciting. The aftermath in the clinic and the mourning in the villages for lost husbands and sons was not so glamorous.

Once, when we had a warrior in the clinic recovering from wounds, a truck load of Kenya army soldiers pulled into the compound and hit the ground running toward the clinic. We two panicked missionary women alone at the mission that day frantically tried to think of a way we could save the guy in the clinic from being taken into custody in his fragile condition. While we were panicking, the soldiers ran back to the truck, without a prisoner, climbed in the truck and left. We rushed to the clinic to see what had happened to our patient, only to find that the troops had come for penicillin shots for STDs and had no interest in our wounded warrior. Such was life in Pokot.

In one incident when I happened to be alone at the mission station while the men were out on a well drilling site, there were again rumors of an impending raid. I was in our house above the mission compound with my usual group of little polio kids who lived at the mission and camped out with us most of the time. We all sat on the deck of the house and watched as people began leaving the mission. Finally we were all alone in a very silent deserted mission station. No fires on the hillsides. No sound of cow bells or the normal clanging of the pumps at the wells. Just silence. When these incidents happened the Pokot warriors always tried to reassure us and to make sure we were protected. Some of them came to tell me that they had warriors down in the dry river bed watching and if the raiders came close they would signal and someone would tell us to run. Of course, none of the polio kids could run and there were too many to carry. I had a vehicle, but being on the road would have made me a sitting duck if the raiders ran across us en route. So we waited and prayed. As we sat on the deck, the kids finally went to sleep but for me there was no sleep that night.

About midnight one of the older school boys came up to the house to reassure us. He had an AK rifle and said he would sit down in front of the house and if the warriors sent the signal that the raiders had been sighted, he would come and tell us. Lotuu sat alone all that night under a tree in front of the house. I knew he was putting himself at risk being there alone, but I was touched and comforted by his faithfulness. About dawn he heard the bird call signal that all was clear and he disappeared as silently as he had come. He later became a notable warrior himself and ended up part of the Uganda army. I will always remember his loyalty and care for us on that scary night.

> The Lord is good, a stronghold in the day of trouble; and
> He knows those who trust in Him (Nahum 1:7)

> I sought the Lord, and He heard me, and delivered me from
> all my fears . (Psalm 34:4)

Dick talks to a group of warriors at the foot of *Kara Suk Hills*.

A warrior who has killed an enemy in battle earns his warrior scars that
give him status and privilege in the tribe for the rest of his life.

# Chapter 18

# The Pokot Women

She rises while it is yet night, and provides food for
her household...She girds herself with strength and
strengthens her arms...She watches over the ways of her
household, and does not eat the bread of idleness.
Proverbs 31:15a, 17, 27

The Pokot women:
resilient...tough...feisty..
always a quick sense of humor
and a zest for life, in the face of
the hardest of times and the most
difficult lives one could imagine.

Polygamous marriage is an interesting arrangement. The first wife is
always the boss of all the wives. Sometimes she will nag her husband to
get another young wife to do the hard work much like we would ask for
a new washing machine or vacuum cleaner. Of course there is jealousy,
especially if the husband shows favoritism for the younger wife. The loud
brouhaha that broke out every once in a while could be heard for quite a
distance. Sometimes the husband would interfere and beat the offending
wife. Sometimes he would just leave them to sort it out among themselves.

One afternoon we heard a big ruckus going on in the village. Down
the path came our neighbor dragging one of his wives behind him. He

had been a renowned warrior who had accepted Jesus and was trying to live by the teachings, but sometimes it was just hard. He came to the door of Pastor John's house and threw the offending wife into the front room. "Here," he said, "If I can't beat her then you deal with her." The "her" was Grace, one of the older wives. Grace was a Christian but notorious for her feisty temperament. The story was that a younger wife had spent the day cooking beans for the husband's guests. As the meal was almost ready to be served, Grace came to claim her borrowed cooking pot. Of course it was the pot that held the beans to feed the visitors. Grace dumped the beans out on the ground and stomped home with her pot. Pastor John had some serious teaching to do with Grace about submission and respect. Later she was moved to her own compound away from the other wives.

A small gourd serves as a water bottle for the baby. The
women are very resourceful, using carved wooden dishes
and gourds for utensils and goat skins for clothing.

Aluminum neck rings, ear rings and lip plugs, a sign
of family wealth for a married woman.

The lip plugs, worn by the older women, are seldom
seen in the younger generation.

An important concept in our ministry was not to change the Pokot culture or to "westernize" the people. I so admired the women and how they utilized what little they had to enhance their lives. They carved bowls and utensils out of wood and grew gourds for water and milk containers. The goat skin skirts with the hair scraped off were tanned and supple, with fancy pleats sewn into the back hem line. The inside of the pleats were made of white-haired goat skin. The result when they walked was a swishing, swinging row of pleats that danced along behind them. A fancy designer could not have made anything more engaging. They were adept at swinging the pleats, especially when they danced.

One day a young woman came and asked me for the denim skirt I was wearing. (I had learned early on that my jeans created confusion among the women about my sexual identity so I switched from Levis to denim skirts.) When she asked for my skirt, I launched into my usual spiel about how practical her goat skins were for sitting on the rough ground and resisting the ever-present thorns that would rip holes in cloth skirts. She listened patiently and then said, "If you like my goat skin so much, then you wear it and give me your skirt." She went away happily wearing my denim skirt and I still have her goat skin, which has often graced our mission display.

The girls gathering for a dance, sporting their "designer" goat skin skirts with white pleats and trim.

*Otieng:*
*"Why do we get so old and you stay young?"*

I can't remember the first time I met Otieng. I have a photo I took of her as a young teen with her circumcision group when she came to sing for us during their version of "trick or treat" when the circumcision candidates can go house to house collecting gifts. I think I gave them shilling coins. I can't remember. But there she is in the photo; her face is painted white and she wears the traditional dark garb of the circumcision ritual. I didn't know her then but I'm sure she was one of the brave ones who did not cry out when they carved her flesh and "made her a woman." Otieng was a plucky one. She fought against the bride price system and won a short battle but in the end she was swallowed up in the culture which did not let women win in the long haul. But I'm getting ahead of myself.

Once, in the early years, as we were preparing to go up country for supplies, a young warrior came begging us to bring him a part for his gun. He was a nice-looking young man, despite having one bad eye. He was a leading warrior and that gave him hero status in the tribe. But his gun had a problem. He needed a spring and knew that we could buy it for him in the city. However, guns were outlawed by the government and we did not feel right helping a warrior who would use the gun on cattle raids. As we drove out of Kiwawa, he cut across to the road and flagged us down to ask us again. Again we refused. I remember him standing there in the road holding the broken gun as we drove away. It was the last we saw of him. He was killed in a battle with the Karamajong shortly after that. He was Otieng's first husband.

It was after that, Otieng, now a young widow, came looking for work. I suppose partly out of guilt that we had not helped her husband, I hired her to help me around the house. It was the beginning of a great friendship that spanned many years and many events of her life. She spoke no English and I was struggling with the difficult Pokot language, but we managed to communicate and to share stories and laughs and later the tragedies of her life. She had that wonderful strength and resilience that I so admired in the Pokot women and she had a crazy sense of humor that often left us weak from laughter

Otieng was an orphan, so her uncle was her guardian with the right to sell her and collect the bride price. Since she was young and strong and pretty, she would bring many cows into his herds. And so the bargaining began. Unfortunately, the men who had the most cows to offer for her were the old grisly men, and she would have no part of that kind of marriage. These old guys already had many wives and sons and they had collected huge herds through the sons' raiding parties to bring back cattle. Having been married to a young warrior, Otieng was not ready to be sold to "a dried-up old man." So the running away began. She spent much time hiding in the bush, where no food and little water were available to her. Once when the Kiwawa school sports team walked to a neighboring village for games, she followed along and was able to beg some food from the girls. It was a hard time for her. I tried to intervene to pay the bride price to free her, but it was 30 cows, which was more money than I could raise.

One day in the midst of this drama, we were sitting in the semi-darkness of pastor John's little mud house, with the old uncle and a group of village elders, trying to mediate the issue on Otieng's behalf. She had been beaten by her uncle and had big red welts on her back and arms. At one point in the meeting, I spoke up and the uncle turned and swung his stick at me and said to Dick, "Control your woman or she will be the next one beaten." Everyone laughed at the thought of the *mzungu* (white) woman being beaten, but for the uncle this was serious business. He had lost several good deals for cows because of her running away and her stubborn refusal of these old suitors.

At last we managed to get an agreement for her to work in the home of our doctor and to give the uncle part of her wages. We thought we had settled the matter. But one day, when the doctor and his family were away, a group of armed warriors came and surrounded the house. Otieng had been sold again and they were coming to claim their father's property. Much posturing and talking followed, but eventually the warriors stormed the house to take her. They searched and searched but could not find Otieng. Finally they left and we went into the house to look for her. High up in the rafters of the ceiling was a stainless steel water tank that could be pumped full from the bore hole to provide water for the house. As we called her name, a little voice came from inside the water reservoir. To this day we don't know how she scaled the walls and got into the tank. But one more time she escaped an unwanted marriage.

Eventually the uncle came up with a younger warrior who had the cows to purchase her. She moved to Uganda and we lost contact with her for many years. She gave birth to seven children; but only four survived. When we crossed paths with her again, she was no longer the beautiful young girl we remembered. She looked at me and asked that question that burned in my heart: "Why are you still young and I am now old?" I cried as I answered her that it was because of the hard life she had lived. Her back was covered with scars from beatings from her husband. I knew that her plucky defiant nature had probably contributed to some of the beatings.

To feed her children and pay their school fees she had been doing the hard work of making charcoal to sell. She cut trees and put them under piles of earth to smolder while the wood turned into charcoal, which she sold along the road to truck drivers to take to the city to sell for household cooking. She managed to put her oldest son through school this way, and he got a job so that he brought her money weekly to buy food for her survival.

Then, some time later, the Karamajong raiders came and took some of the family's cows. This son, the one bright spot in Otieng's sad life, had gone with the other men to reclaim the cattle. As they chased the Karamajong warriors he was in the front of the other young Pokot men as they were chasing the stolen cows, and one of his own group accidently shot him from behind. This final blow of fate took from Otieng the one thing she had to cling to. The next time we saw her she was a broken old woman. We prayed that she would not give in to the alcohol use that so often was the escape for older women whose lives were barren of comfort and joy.

The last visit I had with Otieng, she made the long eight mile walk out of Uganda to come see me at Kiwawa. She had with her a daughter and a beautiful new granddaughter, the chubbiest Pokot baby I had ever seen. There was some of the old shine in Otieng's eyes as she held this new little life. I was deeply touched that she had come to share with me this new joy in her life. We hugged and laughed and remembered the old days when life was full of promise. And here, in her arms, was a new little life full of promise and hope.

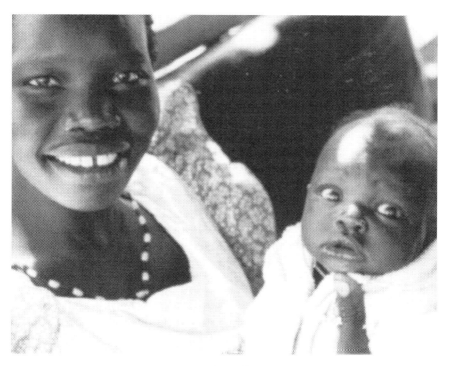

Otieng with her first baby

Otieng, second from right, in circumcision garb.

Otieng in center of picture with her circumcision age mates.

Jane Hamilton

*Female Circumcision*

The Kenya government has been doing a vigorous campaign against FGM, female genital mutilation, as they call it. We know it as female circumcision. We tried unsuccessfully for many years to discourage this practice. It is deeply entrenched in the Pokot culture, as it is in many African tribes. Not only is it a difficult rite for young girls, but it creates scar tissue that makes child birth more difficult and often necessitates cutting of the scar tissue during birthing.

The young girls look forward to their circumcision because of the special status they enjoy during the rites. Faces are painted with white chalk, dark ceremonial cloaks are worn and they go house to house (hut to hut) in the villages singing and asking for treats. It is a time that the older women give them instructions on womanhood and marriage. Most importantly, it recognizes them as a woman and makes them eligible for marriage. It is an important rite of passage for the girls. Celebrations are held; milk and honey are shared with the many visitors who come to the father's home to honor the girls with singing and feasting. A special hut is built for the girls where they will spend several months in seclusion while they heal. Bravery during the cutting is important to the girl's reputation. The brave girls bring honor to their fathers. The girls who flinch or cry out bring disgrace on their fathers and will not be regarded by the young men as good choices for marriage.

The deep significance this has in tribal life makes it very difficult for change to take place. It is all part of coming-of-age, status in the tribe, and marriage prospects for the girls. The government campaign is aimed at girls who are now being schooled and the hope is that by the next generation the practice will have passed away as part of the old history and folk lore of the tribe, but out in the remote tribal areas, it is still a very important part of life for Pokot girls.

Dick with circumcision girls dressed as warriors

Jane Hamilton

Circumcision girls with white painted faces so their fathers won't recognize them; the capes are special for the ritual.

This coming of age rite is a time for the girls to go through the villages receiving gifts and treats and a time for learning from older women about their role in Pokot society.

*The Spit Blessing*

A traditional blessing among the older Pokot, especially the old women, was to spit upon the person being blessed. This was a blessing for new babies but also for anyone you wanted to honor or thank. In the early days we got used to this and realized it was an acceptance of us and a welcoming, even if a bit unhygienic. Over the years as the culture changed, it was done less and less, but in 2011, I was visiting with an older woman at a site where a well was being repaired. She began to explain to me that she was the grandmother of our friend and Member of Parliament, Sam Pogishio. I was questioning this information when one of the young Pokot guys came to my aid to explain that she was a mid-wife who helped deliver him, not the biological grandmother. She was quite elderly and as we talked she explained that it was hard for her to digest the food available in the village and she needed a few shillings help. I gave her a small shilling note, at which she spit on her hand and began rubbing it on my chest. It had been a long time since I had that blessing and it kind of took me back. The young man laughed and said at least she had lived to old age so she probably didn't have TB or anything serious. We all laughed, but somehow I felt a little nostalgic that the old ways were passing away and with it some of the warmth and openness of the Pokot society.

A Pokot grandmother repairs the wall of her house. Grandmothers play an important role in Pokot culture, taking care of the children and passing on the traditions and heritage to the girls in the family. Note the mud roof, keeping out sun's heat.

# Chapter 19

## Is There Power in the Blood?

> Brethren, if anyone among you should wander from the
> truth, and someone turns him back, let him know that he
> who turns a sinner from the error of his way will save a
> soul from death and cover a multitude of sins.
> James 5:19

There was an old man at Kiwawa whose life was forever changed by the gospel of Jesus Christ. His name was Loitaluk. He was the headman of the village and one of the first to come and welcome us to Pokot territory. When Dick first stopped to look at the broken well at Kiwawa, Loitaluk and the other elders came with the pump parts they had buried in the ground so that no one would make spears out of the pipes. The well had been broken for a long time but they had kept the pump parts saying they knew someday someone would come to fix their well. This display of responsibility was one of the reasons we decided to make our permanent mission at Kiwawa.

Loitaluk was the first to bring his children to the school and later to bring his wives and children to the church, but he put off many years becoming a Christian. He liked the beer parties that are so much a part of Pokot men's gatherings. He had been a warrior in his younger days, and so he sat in the council that planned the cattle raids and laid the battle plans. Even though he was chairman of the school committee and attended church regularly, he resisted surrendering his life to the Lord. But one Sunday the Lord moved Loitaluk to stand up at the end of the church service and say that he wanted to become a Christian. Everyone cheered when Loitaluk came up out of the waters of baptism. He was somewhere in his sixties and had lost all but two of his sons in tribal warfare. One of them was killed by Karamajong raiders the day that I had to flee to the hills with the women and children at Kiwawa. Loitaluk at one time had 12 wives; six of his own and six he inherited from a brother who had been killed. He had outlived most of his wives. His had been a hard life, but he had the wisdom of those hard years.

*The Hard Question*:

One Sunday at the end of the communion service, Loitaluk stood up and said he had a question: "Which is stronger, the blood of Christ or the blood of the Sapana sacrificial cow?" he asked. He was searching for an answer to this question because he had seen some things that he could not understand.

In his background he understood the blood of the sacrificial cow. It was powerful and it worked. And this is the way that it worked. When boys become of age to join the ranks of the warriors and become men, they go through a ceremony called *Sapana*. The group of young men who go through this rite together become like blood brothers. Through their whole lives they are a mutual support group. They help each other with obtaining wives. They share their belongings. They give freely to each other. They are a unit. They support each other in all things. They go into battle together and are responsible for each other. They watch each others' backs. If one falls in battle his age mates carry him on their backs. No one would abandon a Sapana brother in battle. They will literally give their lives for each other. And what binds them together are the oaths taken and the blood of the cows that are killed at the Sapana ritual. The pieces of the cow are laid out in ceremonial fashion and they walk between the pieces of the cow. (Isn't it interesting that we find this same oath-taking ritual recorded in the Old Testament in Genesis 15:12-20?).

Loitaluk had been a warrior all his life. He had been a Sapana brother. He had gone into battle and protected his brothers as they had protected him. He knew what it meant. He knew that if two Sapana brothers had a quarrel, the elders of the village would call them together; a cow would be sacrificed and the matter would be settled, never to be spoken of again. Never again could they mention it or even remember it against each other. It was not allowed. The survival of the group, and of the whole tribe, depended on the fighting units. No division could be allowed among them. They had to be bound together. The drinking of the blood of the sacrificial cow bound them together.

Loitaluk's question about the blood of Christ had arisen because he assumed that the blood of Christ would bind Christian brothers together in the same way that the blood of the Sapana cow bound together the age mates. But he saw division and quarreling and gossiping against each other, even among the missionaries. His words to the congregation that morning were, "Those of us who take communion together are like the Sapana group who eat the feast together. That communion feast makes us one. There should be no quarreling or division among us."

What Loitaluk was saying is that we are brothers, bound together, inseparable, to support and help each other, to go into battle against the enemy together, to watch each others backs, to rescue each other if necessary, and to carry a brother on our back if he needs to be carried. Does the blood of Christ bind us together that strongly? When we see a Christian brother fallen, do we pick him up and carry him until he is strong enough to stand again? Or do we run off and leave him alone? Do we jump on him and get in a few blows ourselves with our gossip and our condemnation? A beautiful African Christian lady once told me that only Christians shoot their own wounded. When a Christian brother has fallen wounded by Satan, other Christians in their self-righteousness will often deliver additional blows to their brother. Where is our brotherhood in Christ? Where is our love? Do we recognize who the enemy really is, or are we quick to decide that the enemy is our brother? Oh, what we could learn as Christians about who the enemy really is and how necessary our unity is to the battle we are involved in. Satan has divided and conquered us for so long. And the blood of that perfect sacrifice was shed so that we could be ONE.

Is the blood of Christ strong enough that our differences can be forgotten at the site of the shedding of blood? Can we go out from the sacrifice, from the communion table, as brothers, never to remember our hurt feelings or cross words again? It works for the Pokot because they believe that it works. There is no power in the blood they shed except in their belief that it works. We, as Christians, have the real power in the shed blood of Jesus, the perfect sacrifice. Can we make it work? Or do we make it a mockery of what Jesus did for us?

Praise God, there are those in our Christian fellowships who are into healing wounds and binding up hurts. We are so grateful for those precious Christian brothers and sisters who stand by us during trying times. We know the feeling of having a brother protecting our back in times of attack. Yes, the blood of Jesus does wipe away past sin. Yes, there is power in the blood. Yes, there is healing and restoration and wholeness provided by Jesus' blood. Yes, we do have brothers who are willing to carry us when we are wounded. Praise God!

> Brethren, if a man is overtaken in any trespass, you who are spiritual restore such a one in a spirit of gentleness . . . Bear one another's burdens and so fulfill the law of Christ. (Galatians 6:1-2)

> But why do you judge your brother? Or why do you show contempt for your brother? For we shall all stand before the judgment seat of Christ. (Romans 14:10)

> Don't grumble against one another, brethren, lest you be condemned. Behold, the judge is standing at the door. (James 5:9)

A Sapana group – brothers for life – go through initiation rites
together and form a strong fighting unit in battle.

Loitaluk, as school chairman, supervised placing of the
poles for the first school building at Kiwawa.

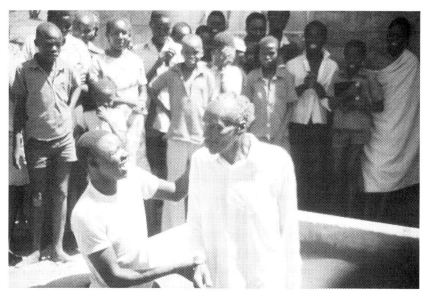

Everyone cheered when Loitaluk came up out of the
waters of baptism, a new man in Christ Jesus.

Dick with the village elders. Loitaluk is fourth from
the left in white shorts and jacket.

# Chapter 20

# African Parables

Casting all your care upon Him for He cares for you.
I Peter 5:7

The Africans are very good at parables. They have for generations passed their history down by stories in the absence of written skills. We were always intrigued by their ability to see irony in situations and to apply life lessons through stories. It made them natural preachers. Even our young evangelists applied this to their teaching and preaching, often with very entertaining results.

*Balancing Act*

Once we were traveling along the Pokot road and passed an old woman carrying a heavy load on her head. Dick stopped the pickup and Benjamin got out to help her into the back of the pickup. We started on down the road and heard peals of laughter coming from the back seat. We turned around to see that they were laughing at the old woman trying to keep the load balanced on her head with every bump and pot hole. Dick pulled over and the guys got out and explained to her that she could lay her load down in the pickup bed. It was her first time in a vehicle. She was used to carrying the load and just didn't think about putting it down. When the guys got back in, these young Pokot evangelists began to discuss how much we are like this with God. He tells us to cast our cares on him and to lay our burden down. We accept his offer and then continue to try to balance our burdens ourselves. We, like the old woman, are so used to carrying our burdens that we just can't put them down and trust Jesus to shoulder the load. When we reached the village of the woman, she kept thanking and thanking us and laughing with the guys about the balancing act. Sometimes when we passed by the village she would run out and flag us down just to have a ride down the road. It always reminded us about casting our cares on Jesus.

*Branded*

The Pokot not only need their herds for survival, they also love their cattle. They treasure the special bulls that are distinctive in some way. They painstakingly shape and curve their horns as they grow. They even make up songs to sing about their cows. It is part of what makes the cattle raiding such a devastating thing for them. The loss of their livestock is always a cause of grieving and sometimes a sentence of death for the family.

Because of the constant threat of cattle raids they have devised a system of integrating their herds with the livestock of other clan members. That way one man's cattle are not all in one location that could be taken by raiders. If a herd is stolen, the family still has cattle in other herds to sustain them. It is kind of like diversifying your investments so a down turn doesn't completely wipe you out.

"But how do you sort them out?" I asked. "We KNOW our own cows!" they replied emphatically. "But with hundreds of cows, how can you know them all?" The *mzungu* (white person) was asking silly questions again. "We just know," they said. And they did. They knew each and every cow. When it comes time to sort out the herds, there is no problem. Like Jesus separating the sheep from the goats. They know their own.

The Pokot goats are often marked with notches on the ears or some other brand that will identify their owner. One Sunday we were visiting the church at Losam and Pastor Paul gave a powerful message from Ephesians 1:13-17 on being "sealed with the Holy Spirit." He was explaining to the congregation that God marks us like the Pokot mark their goats. He talked about us being "stamped." (We always joked about how the British and Kenyans need to have everything stamped with an official rubber stamp, from receipts to government papers.) Paul's illustration was right on. He said that the mark that God stamps us with is the Holy Spirit and he can recognize us and claim us by that mark. When it comes time for God to sort out his herd, He will know us by the Holy Spirit in our lives. People in Paul's congregation were nodding their heads. They understood. God knows His own.

I was thinking about how the Pokot men love their cows and know each one. That is how God is with us. He knows us by name and He knows His own.

Pastor Paul took his message one step further. He added that like looking at the goats' markings everyone knows who they belong to. So everyone who looks at us should be able to recognize who we belong to. They should be able to see Jesus in us. The Holy Spirit marks us so that people can see we belong to God. It was a good analogy for the Pokot who understand very well the "marking" of identification showing to Whom we really belong.

> Having believed, you were marked in Him with a seal; the promised Holy Spirit, who is a deposit guaranteeing our inheritance until the redemption of those who are God's possession – to the praise of His glory, (Ephesians 1:13b)

> . . the sheep listen to His voice. He calls His own sheep by name and leads them out. . . His sheep follow Him because they know His voice. (John 10:3-4)

Pastor Paul preaching about "branding with the Holy Spirit" to his congregation in one of many under-the-tree churches that worship throughout Pokot land

# Chapter 21

# All Things To All Men
# . . To Win a Few

*For to this you were called, because Christ suffered for us,*
*leaving us an example that you should follow in His steps.*
I Peter 2:21

A young mother in our family once came into her kitchen to find that her toddler had drunk some unknown liquid from a jar under the sink. Because the child was too young to tell what effects the drink had, the mother grabbed up the jar and took a big swig of the liquid herself. This became a family joke in later years...this impetuous young mother who might have sentenced herself to the same deadly fate as her child had the liquid been poison. Thinking further through, you have to realize that this mother put herself in the position of the child in order to save it. She could tell the doctor what the symptoms were. The child could not. She would know what was happening in her body to help determine what the liquid was. The child could not. She risked her own life but she did it in order to be in a position to help the child who was completely helpless.

Isn't this so much like God coming into human flesh to help us when we are completely helpless to save ourselves? Jesus lived and suffered and went through our human problems in order to be able to show us a way out of our dilemma. He drank our cup. Like the mother who would be able to describe to the doctor the child's symptoms, Christ is able to tell the Father our problems because he has lived through them. He put himself in our place even though it meant his suffering with our sufferings. By becoming like us, He shared with us in a way that could never have been done from the comfort of heaven.

I remember how my relationship with the Pokot women changed after we had to run together to the hills when the raiding Karamajong tribe came shooting their way close to Kiwawa mission. The fact that we had shared that moment of danger somehow made our relationship deepen and take on a new level. They spoke of it sometimes when we sat talking and it seemed to move me from the status of the *missionary* to just a woman with the same feelings and problems that they had, one with them in frailty and vulnerability. It made a difference. We were able to share as friends and comrades because of that incident. They laughed as they told others how they had tied a cloth around my head so that the Karamajong raiders would not see my blond hair as I climbed the hill in flight. They laughed at me for running in the dry streambeds where the going was easier. Didn't the foolish *mzungu* woman know that the enemy warriors would run in the streambeds? But in the laughing and the shared experience was something deep and lasting that would bond us together in a way that I could never have done by being the visiting "missionary."

When I first went to Africa and was teaching in the rural villages around Kitale town, I would go into some of the small villages with circles of thatch-roofed mud huts. Often there was not a chair or a stool in the compound. The Kenyan women, ram-rod straight from balancing heavy loads on their heads, could sit on the ground with legs stretched straight in front of them in a posture that was impossible for me to copy for any length of time. When I would arrive for a meeting and they realized there was no chair, their protocol was that I stood and waited while someone ran to a nearby hut or neighboring village and found a stool or a chair for me to sit on. This seemed ridiculous to me, but it was a matter of propriety. So we played this little game until one day I just sat myself down on the ground with the women and kids. Everyone was embarrassed. Years of Colonial rule had taught them that white women didn't sit on the ground. No one seemed to know what to do, but after a while they quit running to get me a chair. I had crossed a line and it seemed to be easier for them to talk to me and share their lives and their burdens.

Sometimes we all forgot that I was white. One time I went to a track meet with the kids from Kiwawa school and I met a Kenyan headmaster from another school. He asked me, "Don't you feel uncomfortable when you are the only white person in a big gathering like this?" I replied, "But I'm not the only white person: I came with Jennifer." The laughter erupted immediately. Jennifer was our African nurse from the clinic. She spoke perfect English and was my good friend but she was very black. I looked around and realized that I truly was the only white person in a large crowd of school kids and teachers and spectators. It just had not occurred to me. That kind of identification made it much easier for me to share in the lives of the people. In the isolation of the Pokot bush they had not been exposed to the kind of barriers that colonial thinking had created between black and white in the Kenya highlands, but there still was the distance of cultural barriers. Breaking down those barriers made it possible to participate in their lives in ways that otherwise I would never have been permitted to share. It made my life among the Pokot a fascinating and wonderful experience.

*Identifying* sometimes meant having to get my bottom dirty sitting on the ground. Sometimes it meant eating and drinking things that I'd rather not (like their favorite cow stomach soup). I found that participating was worth it for the sisterhood of the Kenyan women whose lives are more difficult than anything I had ever experienced but whose love embraced me with openness, sharing and joy. Maybe we need to be able to identify more with the hurting of this world. Maybe it will mean sharing in some experiences from which we'd rather be insulated, but there is a hurting world out there. Many don't have our advantages. Many really need someone to get in touch with their lives and feel their hurts. They are out there if we look around and if we don't mind getting a little smudged by the world's dirt. There are kids uncared for, teens in trouble, women in bad situations, drug problems, family problems and a lot of hurt in the world, people with needs that we can meet if we are willing to share in their fears and their pain. Christ did it for us. Are we willing to put ourselves in others shoes and reach out to them? A hurting world needs the healing balm of Jesus that we have locked up in our churches. As Christ's hands and feet, we need to get out there and spread it around.

*Who, me, Lord?*

If you wonder how you can be used by the Lord, have no fear. God can use you in ways you wouldn't dream of. I started out thinking I was a total misfit for bush mission work. What could a public relations secretary possibly do in the bush of Africa? After the famine we enrolled over 600 village children in World Vision sponsorship and I found myself writing out the letters from the children to their sponsors, taking their photos, reporting on their lives and doing the grant reports. There I was, a functioning secretary in the bush. Who knew? Well, God did. The old saying is "God is more interested in your availability than your ability." Just be available and see what God can do with you.

> I have become all things to all men that I might by all means save some (Corinthians 9:22)

Working with a translator to write a child's letter to his World Vision sponsor in USA, one of 600 sponsored kids.

My first contact with women, behind Pastor Andrew's house
where they came to use the hand grinder to turn their maize into
corn meal (traditionally done by grinding between rocks).

Love me . . . love my camel.

Over the years the fashion changed from goat skins to cloth, from bulky aluminum necklaces to softer plastic beads. The tightly spun hair with cow fat and sparkling mica morphed into corn rows. The women always take pride in their colorful adornment. The beauty of strong spirits and zest for life shines out of those faces masking the difficulty of their lives.

# Chapter 22

## Gotta Love God's Creatures

God made the beasts of the earth according to their
kind, the cattle according to its kind, and everything that
creeps on the earth according to its kind. And God saw
that it was good.
Genesis 1:25

"Mom, that's the ugliest baby I've ever seen." In the darkness I had to agree with Carolee. That really was an ugly baby slung on the women's back in the traditional kanga cloth that served as a nesting place for African babies for the first year of their lives. When the one dim light bulb suspended over the generator came back on after the film ended, we looked closer and were surprised to see that the "ugly" baby was really an infant baboon. It seems the mother baboon was killed raiding the corn field and the baby was an orphan. We *oohed* and *aahed* until the women offered to sell it to us for about fifty dollars.. We declined. The last thing we wanted was a wild out-of-control baboon, like the ones we had encountered in the bush. When she unwrapped it from the kanga cloth, we saw there were rope burns around its middle from being tied up. Infection had already started to set in. When the price came down to twenty five shillings (about three dollars) we accepted the little bundle for strictly humanitarian reasons, not to mention the pleading of daughter, Carolee, whose nurse instincts were kicking in. So we headed home with one hysterical little misplaced baboon bouncing about and screaming in the back of the car. Reaching the house, Dick decided the best course of action was just to leave her in the car overnight and deal with it in the morning. She was in no mood to be handled.

The next morning, as we cautiously opened the door of the Land Cruiser, we had no idea how we would handle this aggressive little bundle of fur and teeth. We all stood back and waited to see what she would do. Carolee was standing at the back of the crowd around the vehicle. Little "Chewie," as she would later be named, took one look at all of us and made a jump to Carolee, clinging to her for dear life. Thus, Carolee became the mother of one very interesting little creature. She bottle fed her, diapered her, bathed her, and slept with her even though Chewie would inch up over her face at night seeking the warmth of her breath until Carolee would wake smothered and gasping, pulling her back down under the covers, only to repeat it all again throughout the night.

When Chewie's wounds were healed we decided it was time to repatriate her to the wild. We drove out until we found a troop of baboons and parked close by. Rolling down a window we gently placed her out of the car. She begged to get back in. We waited. She clung to the car, hanging upside down from the roof rack with her little face looking into the windows for some sign of help from her "troop." We waited and waited but no baboon approached her and she was not going anywhere near them. Dick decided the best thing to do was to put her down and drive slowly away in hope that she would connect with the troop. Jumping back onto the roof rack, she began to scream and Carolee and I began to cry. Needless to say we went home with a new member of our family, the beginning of years of entertainment and craziness.

Carolee was always the mother figure, Dick was the head baboon and Rick, being a male, was an accepted authority figure. It turned out I had no place in the pecking order except at the bottom. If Chewie (who was named after the *Star Wars* Chewbacca) would get in trouble in the house for pulling up plants, taking a bite out of every fruit in a bowl or just plain delinquency, she would always react to a scolding by running to bite me. No matter who did the scolding, I was the recipient of the bite. They weren't serious bites, but then she was only a baby. One night she got in trouble in the living room and Rick said, "Mom, you have to establish dominance before she gets any bigger." So as she lumbered across the floor to give me the ceremonial bite, I took off my rubber flip flop and slapped her across the face. She reared back in unbelief and then lunged forward to right this indignity. She clamped her little teeth solidly on my thumb and looked directly into my face as she applied pressure. Dick and Rick rushed to my rescue and it took both of them to pry her from my throbbing thumb. It was the last time I stood my ground. From then on, Chewie ruled the house. Carolee and the guys could discipline her but my place was the cowering troop member who tried not to ever cross her. We settled into a kind of truce so long as I kept my place.

Once as I was mixing up a chocolate cake, she wandered into the kitchen and decided she liked the taste of cake batter. I tried to hustle her out the door but it was no use. Clinging to me, she continued to eat batter until we were both coated with chocolate. By the time Dick came to my rescue, we both needed a shower.

Chewie loved babies and would cuddle them and try to make off with them, much to the parents' dismay. She was very gentle but we had to make sure she never had the opportunity to snatch babies.

As Chewie grew she became more aggressive to strangers and more protective of our property. It was obvious we were going to have to restrain her somehow. A big cage was built where she could be contained when other people were around. She still ruled the roost from inside her cage. Her favorite trick was luring people close to the cage by ignoring them until they got close, and then with precision grip, a lightening strike through the bars of the cage would flick a pen out of a pocket or glasses off a face. When the unsuspecting victim bent over to pick up their item, those little hands would grab two handfuls of hair and jerk their head into the cage bars. She never really hurt anyone but it was a game she thoroughly enjoyed.

The things she could do from inside the cage were amazing. She definitely premeditated her actions. Our regular visitors made friends with her but she still did her mischief. Once a visiting missionary wife was standing next to the cage reading a financial print out from her donors in the states. Chewie grabbed the paper out of her hands, and from Karen's reaction Chewie knew she had a prize. She perched there in her cage, looking into Karen's face, tore the printout into strips, and ate the whole thing one strip at a time. Another time a visitor was doing her wash and got too close to the cage on the way to the clothes line. Oh boy, a prize snatch was a rather large size bra belonging to a very shy person who begged and pleaded to get her item of clothing back. The more she begged, the more Chewie knew she had a treasure. Finally, much to the owner's embarrassment, Dick had to come and get in the cage to retrieve it. Chewie loved these little encounters and waited patiently for her next victim.

When she would be out of the cage playing with us and one of the Rhodesian Ridgeback hounds would come flop on the blanket, we never knew how to get the intruders off; but Chewie did. A quick pinch and twist of a nipple would send the dogs howling off. She had so much savvy. She was jealous of Dick and Rick and anytime a female would touch one of them she would scream as if to say, "hands off my guys." So, of course, the gals would do it just to get her reaction. Once Rick came riding in with a Peace Corps girl on the back of his motorcycle and Chewie went crazy. We warned the girl not to get too close to the cage but she rushed up to pet "the cute monkey." Before we could intervene, the glasses and hair trick had gone down and the head went into the cage bars with a little more gusto than usual.

Chewie's favorite thing was *grooming*. She loved it when Rick would lean against the cage and she could dig through his hair looking for all those little cooties, smacking her lips and making soft contented noises. She could do that for hours. It was her social time. Even though she did not like the big dogs, she loved the little terrier who would sit next to her cage for his grooming time.

I always thought that if I was alone and robbers came, I would run and get in Chewie's cage for protection. The Africans had a natural fear of baboons and could never understand our attachment to her.

At the end of many wonderful years of life with us, she developed a sore on her bottom. Carolee feared it was cancer as it grew bigger and bigger. She would back up and let Carolee doctor it as if she knew that Carolee was trying to help. The sadness in her eyes and her declining health was a very difficult time for the family. When she left us, we had a little funeral and buried her wrapped in a blanket. Again, the Africans could not understand those kind of feelings for an animal, especially one that was a bane of their existence. For us, Chewbacca was one of the special gifts that God gave to us during our years in Africa

Chewie accepted us as her troop and Dick was the head
baboon who could always control her antics.

"Mama" Carolee and Chewie, with one jealous little dog.

Jane Hamilton

Chewie's favorite thing was "grooming" and Rick was her favorite subject.

"But I don't want a bath."

Chewie provided hours of fun and entertainment, along with
some wild and crazy episodes of *monkey business.*

As Chewie grew into an adult baboon, with a dislike of visitors,
a big cage was built for her. But she still ruled the compound
from inside the cage and gave us years of companionship.

Rick spent hours riding the back roads out across the desert, exploring the Northern Frontier of Kenya. His personal ministry was the repair of Pastors' motor bikes. Kenyan pastors would come from miles to have *"Kijana"* (the kid) work on their bikes

A Pokot mama wants to look at herself in the mirror of Rick's motorbike. (Don't know what the guy with the knife wants.)

Rick, with one of his projects, part Toyota and part Chevrolet;
it was affectionately known as the *Toylette*.

Yoda, our nocturnal bush baby, kept our nights lively bouncing
off the walls and delivering little nibble love bites

# Chapter 23

# Pages From the Diary and Other Memories:

> ...be content with such things as you have. For He
> Himself has said, "I will never leave you nor forsake you"
> Hebrews 13:5b

*Snakes and Witchdoctors*

Snakes and witch doctors were the focus of a lot of the questions we were asked when we were stateside on furlough. Snakes we saw plenty; witchdoctors only a few. Sorcerers were the bad guys who cast spells, healers were the ones who did sacrifices for sickness, and the diviners foretold the future by reading the intestines of sacrificed goats or reading the positions of tossed sandals. The ability to do these things was usually passed down in families from generation to generation.

Our encounters with witch doctors and sorcerers were rare. Once the village erupted in panic as the women and children picked up stones and sticks to chase an old woman. She looked harmless enough but people were obviously afraid. We were told that the old woman was a sorcerer and she had been collecting dirt from the entrance of the church to use to cast a spell on everyone who walked over the dirt to enter the church.

People believed in the spells so much that cursed people had been known to simply lie down and die. Strangely, they believed that we white folks were immune to the power of the curses. Our first trips into Pokot we crossed burned sacrifices in the road put there to stop the army trucks from passing. The people believed that our "medicine" was more powerful than the witch doctor. Later on our clinics and western medicine proved that to be true. We encouraged the Christians that the Holy Spirit of God dwelled in them and was stronger than any curse, but the old fears were hard to overcome.

Once an old man, very ill with typhoid, was brought to the mission clinic. Before we could treat him an old man appeared on the scene to do a spell over him. He was a witch doctor but he had no painted face or feathers or strange ornaments. He was very ordinary looking and wore a simple brown *shuka* (cloth tied over one shoulder). I would not have known what he was if I had passed him on the trail. He had two rocks that he tapped together over the man's head as he softly chanted. At the end of his little ceremony he threw the two rocks away into the bush, evidently taking the illness away with them. He melted off into the bush and we never saw him again. The patient did recover. Was it the witch doctor's rocks or the clinic's medicine? That debate would go on around the fires at night.

Many patients came to the clinic after the traditional doctor's medicines failed. Babies would be brought in with goat entrails wrapped around their chests from a sacrificed goat and white chalk markings on heads and bodies. Too often the clinic was the last resort and they had waited too long to seek medical help. Gradually the belief in western medicine grew and we saw less and less of the traditional doctor's medicine.

A family, who has visited the local witch doctor, wear the white chalk markings on heads and bodies to ward off sickness.

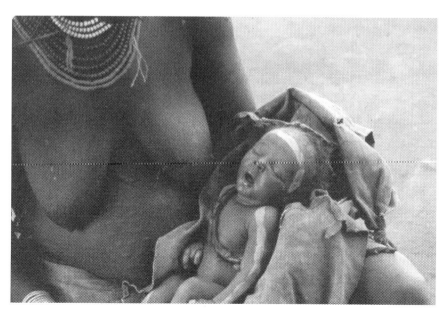

A baby with goat entrails wrapped around its chest from a sacrificed goat to cure illness.

*Dreams*

The people put a lot of stock in the power of dreams. Names and totems were often chosen from dreams. It was believed that if someone was awakened during a dream that his soul would be out "walking" and that he would die if his soul did not get back in him before he awoke. They also believed that special people could foretell the future by their dreams. One of our young evangelists was a son of a chief and the tribe believed that he had the gift of dreams. When he was a very young boy he aroused his family in the middle of the night, saying that raiders were coming. His family fled but the other people in the village did not believe. The village was attacked and many people were killed. From that time the people wanted this young man to train as a diviner, but his choice was to follow his Christian faith.

*The Cobra Who Came to Church*

We were all gathered in the front room of one of the mission houses for a Sunday morning worship time. I was sitting in front of an open window that had the typical big iron mesh to keep out intruders but didn't stop much of anything else. The dog on the porch kept barking and I finally turned around to see what was happening. As I turned, I looked directly into the face of a cobra in full hood, ebony black skin shinning like a new patent leather shoe, with bright yellow stripes, an awesome beauty that took my breath away. Dick grabbed a spear from the wall and we pushed him out on the porch and closed the door behind him, to do battle with the intruder. The cobra measured over six feet. We found out later that it had lived under the house for some time. People knew about the snake but didn't bother to tell the family who had young children playing around the house. Dick felt rather bad about killing it because it was very beautiful, and evidently it had co-existed with people without incident.

Dick with the cobra who came to church.

The danger at the mission compound was that our food storage brought in mice and rats who in turn brought in the snakes. Some of them were spitting cobras and some vipers. Dick killed a big cobra in a storehouse on the compound and decided he needed to see what cobra tasted like. He fried up the little fillets (they tasted somewhat like clam strips). Dick enjoyed every bite but it gagged out all the Pokot young guys standing around watching. He finally persuaded Loupala, the bravest of the group, to try a taste. They don't even eat fish so snake was a big deal. All evening Loupala could feel that snake wiggling around in his belly. It made for a lot of stories told later on.

Snakes often found their way into the outhouses looking for mice. I had the reputation of being really paranoid at night going to the outhouse. People said it looked like a carnival beacon as I shined the light up around the rafters and down around the floor, making sure no creature shared the space with me. Once I went into panic when a giant "bat" was flying about but it turned out to be a small moth on the lens of my flashlight that projected as a giant on the wall. There was a lot of entertainment and sport at my expense but I never did encounter a snake in the outhouse.

Then there was the phantom python that lived near Kiwawa mission. We never saw the snake but the stories said that it left a print as wide as a tire track. They told us when they finally killed it that it took five arrows in the head to stop the giant snake.

## Green Mambas

The most deadly snakes in our area were the green mambas. They are not very impressive looking, like a giant grass snake with a small head and slender body. They can be over seven feet long and live mostly in the thorn trees. Belying their innocent appearance, they are very poisonous. They were nicknamed "ten pacers" because that is about how far you could walk before you were done for. Their paralyzing venom makes it impossible for a victim to breathe.

One memorable encounter was when we were driving to a well site and a mamba crossed the road in front of us. Dick always sped up to try to run over them but they were lightening fast and usually beat us across. On this occasion Dick stopped the car and went after the snake. It was trying to get across a bare patch of ground and into the trees but Dick kept heading it off. When he ran out of rocks he asked the guys to throw him some more rock ammunition from the road. One big rock, poorly thrown, hit him on the thigh and he went down with the snake reared up in front of him. We thought he was a goner. but the snake did not strike. Finally Dick managed to kill it. It was about seven feet long. We took photos of it draped over our necks, etc., threw it in a gunny bag in the back of the trailer and continued on to the well repair site. When we got there Dick was going to show people the snake. Only it was not in the gunny bag. It had crawled out and was in the trailer, very much alive. A second kill made sure it was really dead. Weeks later as we were driving along there was another mamba crossing the road. I did the wifely admonitions about Dick not getting out of the car this time. As we approached the snake, it reared up on its tail and we could see it clearly through the windshield as it did a lightening fast u-turn and plunged back into the bush from where it had come. Dick gasped, "Did you see that?" Of course I had! Dick never again did combat with a mamba.

The "not quite dead" deadly green mamba

The unwelcome snakes came into the mission to eat the rats who came to eat the maize in the storehouses. The obvious solution to the problem was cats! So we introduced a feline defense force into the mission to take care of the rats.

When we would go upcountry for supplies, we would hire school boys to look after the cats. We always left a supply of powdered milk to feed the cats. However, it seemed to the boys that the milk would be much better used to flavor their tea than to waste on the cats. So they hunted birds to feed the cats while they enjoyed tasty cups of African "chai" enriched by the cats' milk powder.

We discovered this when we returned once to find them in the process of feeding a nest of baby owls to the cats. Carolee sprung into action to rescue the one surviving owl, dashed to the clinic to get an eye dropper and baby cereal, and constructed an owl nursery. She named him "Mr. Hiss" and he became a household pet for many years.

Here is an interesting twist to the Mr. Hiss story. The Kenyans were alarmed at our having an owl in our house. Didn't we know that an owl hooting at you meant you were going to die? The strange thing about this superstition was that we had heard it before in a very distant setting. Just prior to leaving for Kenya, we watched a documentary about British Columbia natives who believed the same thing about owls. The program was called: *"I Heard the Owl Call My Name."* It told of people who really believed they would die if an owl called to them. How strange to find an identical belief among animistic people on the other side of the world. We managed to beat the odds and no one died from Mr. Hiss' hooting.

Mr. Hiss was a delightful pet. He would sit on the back of a chair at the dining table and beg food from our plates. If Dick was working at night in the shop, Mr. Hiss would sit on the back of the tool box and visit. He was always free to come and go so he would go out at night hunting and return in the morning to sleep in a little cage we built for him. Dick could always call him in and he would glide so silently you never heard him coming. The only time he wasn't silent was when we sang hymns with a little pump organ and he would screech loudly in accompaniment.

He was absolutely afraid of nothing and that fearlessness eventually led to his demise when he tangled with the dogs once too often and came out the loser. We all grieved the loss of this wondrous creature that had enthralled and blessed us. He was such an unlikely pet but his interaction with us was affectionate and playful. It was not like we "owned" him. He just lived with us and did his own thing. The years he was our house guest, he brought a magical quality to our everyday lives.

Mr Hiss

Mr Hiss, visiting with Dick over the tool box, keeping
him company for some late-night repairs.

Jane Hamilton

*The Elephants*

Over the years we developed a deep love for elephants. Seeing them in the wild is its own kind of epiphany. They are so huge yet so agile, so wondrously social with each other, so full of life in their own habitat that you never again want to see one in a zoo. After encountering them in the wild, you know immediately when you see them in a circus or a zoo that they are seriously depressed.

Our most memorable event with elephants was a visit to a tourist lodge in the Aberdares called *The Ark*. Busses bring tourists to the lodge and people sit up all night watching a lighted water hole as animals come and go. It is one of the best places in Kenya to comfortably view wildlife. Our family was booked in for two days so after the tourists left the morning of the second day, we had the place all to ourselves for the daylight hours. To our delight, groups of elephants began coming in to the water holes. One of the females was in season and we watched as a big male pursued her, charging through the bushes and splashing through the water. Every time they made a pass through the water hole, all the other elephants trumpeted like they were celebrating a party. The pair eventually crashed off through the brush and we didn't see them again.

As the groups would come and go, the mamas would greet and touch the babies in the other groups, like mothers everywhere inspecting newborns. It was like friends glad to be together as they greeted each new group that came in. It was our best day of wildlife viewing, a bonus we had not expected, a little special gift from God for some weary missionaries.

Out on the plains you could drive fairly close to elephant herds and they didn't pay much attention. Dick always tried to drive up close for a photo. He knew that they would do a little charge and flap ears a few times before they got serious about going after you. Good photos resulted from those little warning, ear-flapping charges. One time Dick spotted an old male all alone down in a dry creek bed. That should have been a clue, but Dick got out of the car and climbed down the bank to get "one last film." As he approached the old bull, there was no flapping of ears or warning charges, just moving feet charging directly towards Dick. As Dick scrambled up the bank, the video camera captures ground and sky, ground and sky and my brother Jim saying, "Well, Hamilton, it doesn't take you long to look at an elephant." As we were laughing in the car, the old rouge came climbing up the bank and we quickly started the car to flee. It was one of those things that got funnier with every telling. It was also a lesson learned about old rogue elephants who don't follow the rules.

*Shopping Africa Style - Straining the Gnat:*

There were many ways to shop in Kitale in the early days. There was the city market (the green grocer) where local women sold their garden items. Every price was up for debate (haggling) and your purchase was put in your own sisal shopping bag or wrapped in newspaper. The women would shout out to me as I entered the market area trying to get my business for their individual stall of produce. I had a hard time haggling over a few shillings when I knew the hard work these women put into planting and harvesting and carrying big heavy gunny bags to market, but if you didn't haggle over the price they thought you were not too bright. So Dick would go to Market with me to do the bargaining. Eventually I got on to it and it became a "game" that we all enjoyed. Years later we went to Israel with a tour group from Puget Sound Christian College and we found ourselves bargaining on their behalf for the tourist items in the shops, much to the annoyance of the shopkeepers.

Then there was the Kitale meat market where fresh meat kill was brought every morning and hung in the market and you could point to the cut you wanted and they would shoo away the flies and cut it off for you. Fillet was the same price as the leg. You just made your choice and again it would be wrapped in yesterday's newspaper for you to carry home.

The regular little corner store was always an adventure to see what was on the shelf: maybe canned beans, once in a while canned tuna, usually just the staples of sugar, salt, oil and flour. If there was something new in stock, you grabbed it because it probably would not be there again. A USAID couple stationed in Kitale got a hardship allowance because there were less than three kinds of beans available in the shops. If you got to the market early in the day you could get packets of milk which were delivered every morning but not refrigerated and would be sold out by noon.

Early on I struggled with the supplies from the market. The cardboard boxes were always infested with roaches that invaded your kitchen, but only came out at night. You could walk into the kitchen at night, shine a light, and a black carpet of roaches would scatter back into the cracks and crannies where they hid during the daylight hours. Rick had some sport at night trying to see how many he could surprise and swat before they got away. With no television or radio, what else is a kid to do in Africa?

The flour products were always full of weevils in some stage of development, little white larvae or little winged critters flying to infest something else in the cupboard. In the beginning I sifted my flour and then found that it needed sifting again when I used it. Later when we got a freezer at our base house in Kitale, I would put the newly purchased flour in the freezer to kill the weevils and then would sift as used. Later on I decided the little guys lived their whole lives in the flour and couldn't really be too unhealthy so I froze them and then just used the flour, weevil bodies and all. In the bush with no freezer, we just ate them. No ill effects.

We always looked forward to going to the capital city where there were more things in the stores and we could load up on items not available in Kitale. On the return trip, we would drive through the beautiful Kenya Highlands were everything was lush and green with banana trees and farms. Along the highway would be the women selling veggies, with the best potatoes we ever tasted, carefully piled in square tin cans with the biggest potato forming a peak on the top of the pile. Dick loved the bargaining with these sassy women who would recognize our car and flag us down. Once when they were pouring the purchased potatoes into our sack, Dick noticed cardboard in the bottom of the tin. He grabbed it away and shook out the layers of cardboard in the bottom to make the tin look fuller. The women whooped and laughed and slapped their thighs, that the *mzungu* (white guy) had discovered their trick. We all laughed and got back in the car to continue our trip home. Such was life in Kenya. The worst offense to the Kenyans was when we got "serious" about something. Everything was just a big game and if you were not clever enough to out-wit them, then it was your own problem. But it always had to be done in good spirits.

Back home in America I miss the fresh veggies, the papaya, the mangos, the big heads of cabbage and the wonderfully sweet ripened-in-the-garden pineapple. Sometimes I miss the women at the city market calling out to the *mzungu* lady, vying for my business, and the friendly camaraderie that went with the whole process. Those memories make shopping in USA pretty tame.

Our first furlough home I went into a store alone to buy some things. I was so overwhelmed by the choices and the variety that I fled the store in confusion, unable to make choices. I had to be accompanied back later and walked through the process of American consumerism.

## Africa Calling

Often I am asked what life in Africa was really like. It is hard to explain the everyday magic that is Africa. No two days were ever alike. There was something new waiting to spring on you at every turn. Dick was always enthralled with the nature and wild life that was all around us. He would stop along the road to witness some fascination of nature that the rest of us didn't even notice. Living in the bush with Dick was never boring; there was always something happening. Like all of us squatting in the dirt waiting for the little ant lion to pop out of the trap door and grab its prey. Or the night of the *great gecko battle*. Someone suggested placing bets, but no one anted up. We certainly were not missing TV sports coverage as we sat engaged in the life and death struggle on the stucco wall above our heads. A large praying mantis and a gecko were in an intense wrestle-off that lasted for almost an hour. Eventually, the gecko won and we all felt a little sad for the valiant mantis who gave it a good go.

Every trip in the car was an adventure, with wildlife apt to appear at any moment, in any place. Like the leopard that silently emerged out of the bush, loping beside the car for several miles, the rhythm of its bobbing tail mesmerizing in the fading light, and then disappearing back into the bush, leaving you wondering if you had really seen it or if it had just been a beautiful apparition. The adventure of it has its own kind of *high* that carries you along in its spell. Not one day of our forty years of Africa experience was I ever bored.

## The Magic

Part of the magic of Africa is, of course, the beautiful vast terrain, always awe inspiring, always changing, always inviting, always challenging. Yes, there were always adventures and challenges. And yes, there were snakes and critters. But the wildlife and the snakes were not my Africa, nor were the adventures or the sometimes *interesting* food. Africa, for me, was the *people*: the warm, joyous, "celebration of life" people, who had so little of material goods, but experienced life with such gusto. Their spontaneous singing touched some deep place inside my soul and took worship to a whole new level. Their warm exuberant greetings always touched my heart and the way that they embraced us as a part of their lives and included us in their communal living, later left me feeling lonely and disconnected when I was no longer part of them.

We had been home for a while when I went with my daughter, Carolee, to see the film *Dances with Wolves*. Sitting in that dark theater, watching Kevin Costner's character being accepted into the Indian tribal life, the movie stirred inside of me the memories of all that I missed of life with the Pokot. After the film we sat on a bench outside the theater, fighting the tears that tried to surface, as we did some thoughtful introspection of the strange emotions we were feeling. There is an empty heart space inside of me that may always be hollow and vacant.

*Please don't drink the water*! There is an old saying in Africa that if you drink the water of the river you will always return to that spot. In the years since we left Kenya, the desire to return is always there. In my dreams at night and in my daydreams... always I long to go back ... to the people I left behind, to the wondrous experience of Africa. It always calls to me.

A lot of social life and camaraderie takes place around water wells, where the women gather to pump and fill their jugs.

Warm welcoming greetings, so important in Pokot culture.

Jane Hamilton

Welcoming gifts of beadwork, carved stool and staff, and
the choir singing a wonderful welcome celebration.

Greetings and admiration of the ostrich feather on *mzee's* hat.

*Kogo*

Somewhere along the way I was given the handle "Kogo." It means grandmother. . . not just any old woman but one's own grandmother. I think it was Pastor John Mosonik who first called me that and soon all 600 kids in the primary school were calling me Kogo. It was an honor I accepted with emotion and pride. Today my grown children, grandchildren and great grands all call me Kogo and somehow it found its way on the license plate of my P T Cruiser and my email address. It carries such precious memories of all those little ones over the years to whom I was their "Kogo."

Visiting with the school kids behind our house at Kiwawa.

"Kogo Jane" waiting for the guys to repair a well, always surrounded by an entourage of children.

# Chapter 24

## "The Real World"

Jesus answered, 'My kingdom is not of this world. If My
kingdom were of this world, My servants would fight . . .
but now My kingdom is not from here.
John 18:36

During our first years in the bush we referred to back home as "the real
world." "Wonder what's happening in the real world?" was a common
comment, as we were so isolated from news of the outside world. But the
longer we lived in the bush, seeing life-and-death situations on a daily basis
and living with people for whom survival was a daily struggle, we began to
think that the bush **was** the real world and that many things in the developed
world were simply not based on reality.

Case in point: Returning home to USA for furlough, I was asked to
speak at a women's meeting in a local church. As we sat visiting before
the meeting, some of the women were commenting on a family in crisis.
Mentioning divorce, cancer and teens in trouble, several women expressed
obvious concern about what was happening to this family. So... naïve me
suggested we have prayer for the family. Conversation abruptly stopped
and an embarrassing silence followed as someone tried to explain to me
that they were discussing a soap opera television program. I was the most
embarrassed of all. I wanted to say to them that there is a very real world
out there where third world women lose six out of ten babies. I wanted to
tell about women having to walk miles every day to carry their family's
supply of water; about women listening for gun shots in the night to scoop
up their children and run for the hills to escape cattle raiders; about women
digging into the cement-hard ground to plant their family's hope of harvest
and food, waiting for rains that may or may not come to provide life-giving
sustenance. How can we grieve over Hollywood "reality" shows when there

are so many of God's people around the world facing real day to day "reality" situations? Where is the "real world" anyway? But I didn't say any of those things. I just sat in embarrassed silence at being so out of touch with my culture and my homeland. I realized I had become a pilgrim and a stranger in my own country.

As we pass through life we are so caught up in the here and now. My hubby often reminds me that we are eternal beings passing through a temporary world, and that I need not get so "worked up" about temporary situations. The reality **is** the spiritual realm. This world is passing away and we are just passing through.

The Scripture so aptly says:

> Do not love the world or the things in the world. If anyone loves the world, the love of the Father is not in him. For all that is in the world, the lust of the flesh and the lust of the eyes and the pride of life, is not of the Father, but is of the world. And the world is passing away and the lust of it; but he who does the will of God abides forever. (I John 2:15-17)

> Heaven and earth will pass away but my words will by no means pass away. (Mark 13:31)

> That I may know Him, and the power of His resurrection and the fellowship of His sufferings, being conformed to His death; in order that I may attain to the resurrection from the dead. . . . . For our citizenship is in heaven, from which we also eagerly wait for the savior, the Lord Jesus Christ. (Phil 3:10,11, 20)

> . . .begotten us again to a living hope through the resurrection of Jesus Christ from the dead, to an inheritance incorruptible and undefiled and that does not fade away, reserved in heaven for you. (I Pet 1: 4)

The real world, a thin line of life and death, depending totally on the scarce rain fall, water from the wells and the livestock.

In the "real world", life depends on daily trips to the well.

Precious jugs of water to sustain family life.

# Chapter 25

# God Speaks to Us . . . From His Word . . . in His Time

Let us hold fast the confession of our hope without
wavering, for He who promised is faithful.
Hebrews 10:23

Sometimes God speaks to you in a still small voice. You just know that it is from God, whatever form it takes. A few times in my life I have known that God was speaking to me. We don't usually talk about those times, because they are so personal and because we don't want someone else judging whether that was God or our own subconscious or some circumstance that *just happened.* But ... *whatever!* I know in my heart that a few times I have had a message that was for me at a time when I desperately needed the message.

One of our later trips to Kenya to repair wells was during a very disturbing and heart-breaking time. One of our strongest pastors had decided to enter Kenya politics. In Kenya, like the USA, a political campaign takes a lot of money. His source of money was the church and the mission. He was fighting us over the drilling equipment and the mission assets, and with his political influence he was making things very difficult for us. The thought that he might be elected to a powerful political office made people afraid to cross him, so we were in a tenuous position. I was very discouraged, not knowing if that might be our last trip to Kenya ever.

At the end of our trip, we went to spend a few days at the Masai Mara game reserve out in the Serengeti plains. Two days in the Mara was a welcome relief. There's no place on earth like the savannas of Africa. We especially enjoyed the daybreak game drives, watching the plains come to life in the streaming early morning light: the stately giraffe lumbering along, herds of grazing impala and gazelles, lions returning from the night's hunt crossing the road in front of us (oblivious to the tourists in the Land Rover), an occasional cape buffalo or solitary rhino, and the huge hippos grunting and blowing in the pools along the Mara River. It is one of God's magical places and we began to relax seeing the wonders of His creation in their natural habitat. But still our souls were troubled by the events and the struggles going on with the mission.

At the game lodge we had one waiter assigned to us for all our meals. He noticed us praying at mealtime and told us he was also a Christian. He asked if we would like to go to their evening worship and asked if Dick could bring them a word. After supper we followed him out behind the kitchens, winding our way down a dark path between the staff houses and out buildings. We could see people in their little wood buildings cooking their dinner and guys loitering around. I felt a little uneasy in the dark and unfamiliar surroundings, stumbling along with no flashlight. In fact, as we left the little group of houses and went further into the darkness of the forest, I was saying to myself: "*This is not good.*" I walked closer to Dick on the narrow dirt path, my eyes searching the shadows for any movement. Finally we came around a corner to a small building and we could hear the joyous sound of singing and a keyboard playing. The sign above the door said: "*Jesus Glory Chapel.*" There, deep in the woods, near the compound of the people who daily kept the tourist lodge running, was a little worship chapel. A small group of men, staff of the lodge, were singing and praising God. What a welcome sound there in the darkness of savanna forest.

One of the men, very articulate, beautiful white teeth smile and handsome face, stood up to bring a word from the Lord. He said he was the medical officer for the Lodge, and took care of the medical needs of the staff and visitors. He read one scripture and it was Phil 1:6:

> *being confident of this very thing, that He who has begun a good work in you will complete it until the day of Jesus Christ.*

That was his word from the Lord for the congregation. He read that scripture and he sat down. I just knew it was God's word of encouragement for me on that night. My heart rejoiced that it was His promise for us and it was why He brought us to that little chapel on that night. I'm sure Dick's message was good, but I didn't hear it. I didn't hear another thing. I was holding on to the word that I was sure was God speaking to me, to relieve my aching heart and assure my soul of His presence and comfort.

God did give us more years and has kept His promise to complete the work He began. The young man lost his bid for the political seat. Although the Kiwawa Church was divided by the politics, it survived and the church at large went forward with growing congregations and new little churches being planted, many of them meeting under the trees throughout Pokot Land and worshipping the true and living God. Thousands are being reached with the gospel as an indigenous church brings their own to Jesus.

God is faithful. His word does not return void. He completes His work until the day of Jesus Christ when we will have the joy of rejoicing around the throne of God with Pokot brothers and sisters. God is good and He is faithful.

> Therefore know that the Lord your God, He is God, the faithful God who keeps His covenant and mercy for a thousand generations with those who love Him and keep His commandments. (Deuteronomy 7:9)

# Chapter 26

# His Church Triumphant

... on this rock I will build My church, and the gates of
Hades shall not prevail against it.
Matthew 16:18

Then I saw another angel flying in the midst of heaven,
having the everlasting gospel to preach to those who dwell on
the earth—to every nation, tribe, tongue, and people

Revelation 14:6

Kiwawa, the first and mother church that has grown dozens of village
churches throughout Pokot land. Thousands of baptized believers
are worshipping the true God and following His Son, Jesus.

Proclaiming the name of Jesus in a land where many have yet to hear that name.

A full house for Sunday morning worship at Kiwawa Church.

Jane Hamilton

Pastors praying; hearts accepting Jesus as Lord of their lives.

Part of the greeting circle after worship service at Kiwawa.

Over 200 people lined up this day for baptism. Water is scarce in the desert so all churches come together for baptism day.

Women carry water all day to fill the baptistery for this special celebration of new birth into Jesus.

Visiting Katuda Church

The greeting circle at Nabokotom Church, Uganda.

Most church buildings are made with traditional mud walls but
have corrugated tin roofs to withstand the heavy rains.

Many village churches meet under the trees or shade shelters like this one, lifting
up the name of Jesus as the gospel continues to spread throughout Pokot land.

Jane Hamilton

1978: Pastor John Mosonik, Pastor Andrew Kendagor, a local headman, Chief Timothy Lopongo and Wayne Christian, (Board Member of East Africa Christian Mission), at the site of the new mission station property given by Chief Timothy.

TODAY: Kiwawa Mission, a light in the darkness, shining the love of Jesus into surrounding villages, with Church, Schools, Dormitories, Clinic and store house for distribution of famine relief food and the supplies and food for the nursery schools.

In the 1970s Pastor John Mosonik and Dick Hamilton stood
at the undeveloped mission property, with the first sign board
above on the tree, full of hope for the Pokot church.

TODAY; Sign Board of the current mission, ACCK, Associated Christian
Churches of Kenya, totally under Kenya leadership, the church continues
to reach out with the message of the Lord Jesus Christ and His Kingdom.

# Chapter 27

# Lights of the City Up Ahead

For he waited for the city which has foundations, whose
builder and maker is God.
Hebrews 11:10

We started our ministry to the Pokot as a *Safari Ministry*, going out from a base in the little city of Kitale to try to establish a permanent place in the bush. In those early days the roads were incredibly bad. In the beginning we stayed in tents in the bush with few comforts of home. We would go out on safari and stay for as long as our constitutions would allow. After some weeks we would be thoroughly exhausted, dirty and out of food supplies, and we knew we had to get out for a few days of rest and resupplying. We called it getting "*bushy*" and we knew it was time for a needed break.

We would pack up and make the long drive across the Great Rift Valley floor and climb up the road, carved out of the escarpment wall, to reach the highlands at the top. After hours of bumping along teeth-rattling washboard and jarring potholes with the heat and the flies, we were sooo ready for a hot bath and a cold drink, both of which were non-existent in the bush in those early years. There was no electricity anywhere and by the time we reached the highlands the night was very dark … maybe we'd see a cooking fire once in a while but mostly black, black darkness. At the top of the escarpment we still had an hour ahead of us on the notorious Kapenguria road (before paving). In the dry season the dust was so thick that you had to roll your windows up in order to breathe, no matter how hot it was. In the rainy season the dust turned to slime and you slid all over the slick surface of the wet clay road. Once, some local entrepreneurs were arrested for going out at night digging holes, so they could charge to push people out. Luckily we had a winch and didn't need the pushers.

As we bumped (or slid) along that last stretch of road, far off in the distance we would start to see a faint glow of lights. . . city lights. An old hymn would go through my mind with the words, *"I see the lights of the city up ahead."* The song, of course, was talking about Heaven. Somehow the experience became a life parable to me on those long difficult trips out of the desert. It was the promise of comfort, refreshment and renewal that lay ahead with just a few more miles of bumpy road, aching muscles and dry throats and then the glow of the lights calling us on to the respite we were looking forward to. Oh, those hot baths and cold drinks (with ICE) were just as wonderful as we had anticipated. A crisp salad, fresh fruit and a meal that *wasn't* goat meat, and then a soft bed in a cool room; it was everything I had been longing for on that long ride.

I still think about that parable of life's journey. Sometimes this road of life we travel gets pretty bumpy. Our bodies get older, trials come and losses are suffered. Sometimes the struggle makes us tired. As I get older and the world gets more chaotic I look heavenwards and feel that same longing I used to feel on that dusty road looking at those distant lights. The lights are up ahead of us, where Heaven promises "no more pain, no more sorrow, no more loss." Revelation 21:4 says God will wipe away every tear from our eyes. It's there in the distance. We can see the light of HIS HOLY CITY, the glow that draws us on. The place that Jesus said He was going **to prepare for us.**

> Let not your heart be troubled; you believe in God, believe also in me. In my Father's house are many mansions . . . I go to prepare a place for you. (John 14:1-2)

> But now they desire a better . . . a heavenly country. Therefore God is not ashamed to be called their God, for he has prepared a city for them. (Hebrews 11:16)

> Now I saw a new heaven and a new earth . . .Behold the tabernacle of God is with men, and he will dwell with them and they shall be His people. . . and God will wipe every tear from their eyes; there shall be no more death nor sorrow nor crying. There shall be no more pain, for the former things have passed away. (Rev 21:1,3,4)

The city had no need of the sun or of the moon to shine in
it, for the glory of God illuminated it. The Lamb is its light.
But there shall by no means enter it anything that defiles,
or causes an abomination or a lie, but only those who are
written in the Lamb's Book of Life.(Rev 21:23,27)

God invites those whose names are written in The Lamb's Book of Life
to come and fellowship with Him, to meet Him in the prayer closet and to
walk daily with him in sweet fellowship. . . until that time when we cross
over and we see the lights of that city up ahead, with all of its promises and
all of its joys. The closer we get to "home" the brighter the lights are calling
us on. **It's a great journey.**

**Post Note:** The final chapter of this book is not written because the ripples
in the pond are still going out and for years to come the results of the small
pebble dropped in that pond will be making their influence felt. We stand
on the shore and watch. And we have no regrets.

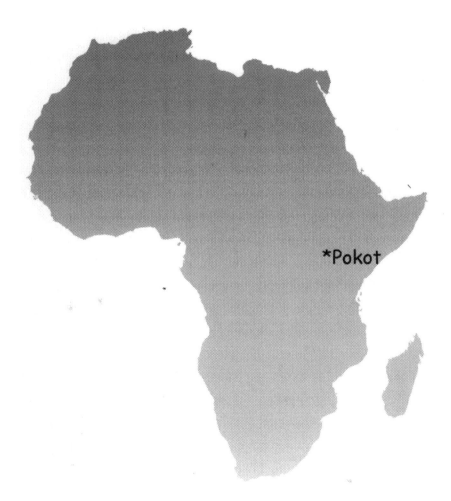

Kiwawa Mission in West Pokot, Kenya, in the Horn of East Africa

Jane Hamilton

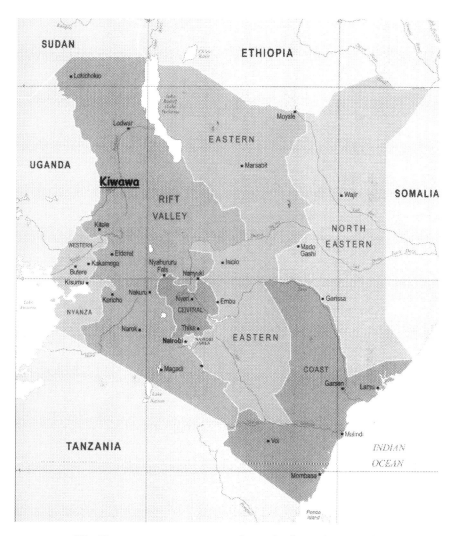

The Kiwawa mission sits just a few miles from the Uganda border in the northern frontier of Western Kenya.

Common Swahili Words:

Bwana Asifwe – Praise the Lord

Chakula - food

Dawa – medicine

Habari – How are you?, What's the news?

    *Response:* Mzuru – good, fine

Hakuna Matata – no trouble

Jambo - hello

Kanisa – church

Kijana – youngster

Mungu – God

Mzee – older man (plural - Wazee)

Mzungu – white person

Shuka – cloth covering worn by men

Watoto – children (mtoto child)

Printed in the United States
By Bookmasters